A users guide to the
WILD & SCENIC
Cache La Poudre River

A comprehensive guide for canoeing,
rafting and kayaking Colorado's only
designated "Wild & Scenic" river.

by Bryan Greene Maddox

This book is dedicated to the memory of

Eric Spradling and Jim Sykes

One taught me the exuberance and enthusiasm of life.
The other taught me that you do not die with dignity and honor,
but that you live with them and they carry on through death.

SPECIAL ACKNOWLEDGEMENTS

Amy L. Maddox, *wife and editor*

George and Betty Maddox, *parents and editors*

Mike Johnson

Christy Alden, *illustrator*

Gary Brunner, *photos & paddle partner*

ACKNOWLEDGEMENTS

Gui Garcia, *cover shot of Bill Taylor*

Amy Maddox, *back cover shot of Bryan Maddox*

Sean Hoff, *Colorado Division of Water Resources*

United States Forest Service

Division of Wildlife

ISBN: 1-881-663-07-8
Copyright © 1993. Revised copyright © 1997
by Bryan Greene Maddox
All rights reserved.
Published by Poudre Canyon Press, LaPorte, CO 80535
Book design by Ann Carr
Printed in Canada

TABLE OF CONTENTS

PART 1: Getting Acquainted

PART 2: The Journey Down the River

PART 3: Accommodations

PART 4: Glossary, etc.

INTRODUCTION

Cache La Poudre means "hide the powder." Several different renditions of a story leave a researcher groping for the true one to publish. Basically, the story is told of French trappers whose wagons were slowed by heavy snowfall. They hid their gunpowder to lighten their load. The cache was later retrieved. The designated cache spot is marked by a small monument just west of Ft. Collins on the west side of the Bingham Hill Road. The river is located northwest of Ft. Collins and runs parallel to Highway 14, a designated scenic byway. The entrance to the canyon is a mile west of the intersection of Highway 287 and Highway 14.

Designated "Wild and Scenic" by the United States Congress, the Poudre is the first and presently only river in Colorado to receive such an honor. To attain this designation, the river had to meet certain conditions. First, it had to be free-flowing. The Poudre met this criteria even though it has eight water-storage units in its headwaters and several diversions to bring water in and to take water out along its mainstem. The river also met the recreational criteria. The United States Forest Service has reported a growth in boating between 1967 and 1977 of 2,000 percent and a regular yearly growth of nearly 30 percent.

However, all is not roses on the Poudre. The Bureau of Reclamation has a dam in the works for the Poudre Canyon. The problem stems from the section that is not protected. The Poudre, below Poudre Park, has no designation. This is where the Pendergrass Dam and Reservoir would be placed.

Another threat to the canyon is the mass of people who come here to recreate. The narrow canyon's facilities can accommodate very little growth, and the road is winding and dangerous. This leaves the Forest Service and the Highway Department struggling to keep the river corridor accessible and safe. The key is respect.

Respect the river. Please leave no trash. Use the bathroom facilities.

Respect people. Watch where and how you park. Don't run over fishermen. Stay out of people's camps and picnic spots. Keep the screaming to a minimum. Stay off private property.

Respect yourself. Know your limits. Have appropriate equipment and emergency gear. Read a quality guide book.

Getting Acquainted:
LOCAL HYDROLOGY

The Cache La Poudre is the only designated "Wild and Scenic" river in Colorado as of this writing. It is also the only free-flowing river on the front range of Colorado. From the headwaters in Rocky Mountain National Park to the confluence with the South Platte in Greeley, Colorado, it is the water itself which makes this river so exceptional. Try to imagine this river with no water. Well, it would hardly be a river at all. Where the water comes from and where it flows always seems to be a topic of conversation among river runners. "Looks like a drought this year." "What's it read on the gauge?" "That rock wasn't there yesterday!" "I heard they are trying to dam the Poudre again. I wonder if Heyduke is in town."

From its headwaters to the plains, the Poudre has many tributaries contributing to its mainstem. However, the "big three" are of most concern to river runners. Nestled in the Kawuneeche Valley in Rocky Mountain National Park, Poudre Lake is the beginning of the Big South fork of the Poudre. This wadable little creek flows approximately 22 miles northeast until it parallels Highway 14. This section is considered "wild" under the Wild and Scenic designation. A beautiful trout stream and alpine riparian habitat, very few people have run this wild section. Following County Road 63E across the Eggers Bridge to the CSU campus at Pingree Park, two reservoirs dump their water into the Little South Fork of the Poudre. This tight and technical run empties into the Poudre near Mountain Park campground. Above the Filter Plant Run is the final tributary that adds water to the Poudre. The North Fork of the Poudre originates in the Cherokee Park area. Cherokee Park is a public access area between Ft. Collins and Red Feather Lakes. This water is stopped temporarily in Seaman's Reservoir before it is dumped into the Poudre.

When you watch the Poudre flow by, you'll notice that it flows with a purpose—to keep municipalities' lawns green, toilets flushed and the agriculture of the Greeley area growing. This water has been fought over and diverted since man entered the valley. The Big South Fork of the Poudre has four storage facilities: Long Draw Reservoir, Barnes Meadow Reservoir, Joe Wright Reservoir, and Chambers Lake. The Little South Fork of the Poudre stores water in Hourglass Reservoir and Comanche Reservoir. Finally, the Seaman's Reservoir holds water on the North Fork of the Poudre.

All of the storage facilities and diversions on the Poudre seem to contradict its free-flowing designation. The main source of water in the Poudre comes from the snowfall in the mountains. As the snow begins to melt in the spring, the river rises. On the other hand, as the snow in the high country begins to run out so does the water in the river. A kayak expedition in October–April will leave the kayakers in ankle-deep water. Beginning in May, the river comes up very quickly. Mid-June signals the historical peak of the river. August's hot days leaves barely enough water to float, and by mid-September the river is once again Poudre "creek."

THE GAUGE

The water cfs readings attained from phone-in river readings are always off for the Poudre. Due to changing diversion amounts, the readings are off between 100 cfs and 800 cfs. On the Poudre this can be 50 percent of the flow. Most Poudre locals know the river flow more by the "rock" gauge. Just upstream of the lower bridges put-in on the north side of the river there is a gauge painted on a rock in fluorescent orange that shows graduated increases in 1/2-foot increments. The hydrograph below shows the corresponding rock readings in feet and corresponds to actual cfs before diversions. This is a more accurate device for gauging the flow and thus is safer.

THE HYDROGRAPH

The hydrograph is a combination of information from Sean Hoff at the Department of Water Resources and Carl Chambers of the United States Forest Service. The High, Medium and Low are references to the section tables found at the beginning of each river segment section. These can be cross referenced to the rock gauge and cfs. The historical peak of the Cache La Poudre is June 15 and the average cfs peak is 2,500 cfs.

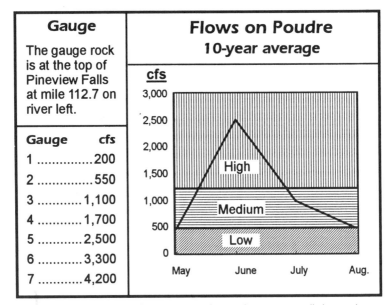

*Due to the fact that the Poudre is a snow melt river, the season usually begins the 1st of May and tapers off in mid-August. This is dependent on seasonal snow pack.

Getting Acquainted:
LOCAL GEOLOGY

As river runners, we experience much more than just the water. The enjoyment of the sport comes from the intimate contact with the environment. The whole environment. The geology of an area greatly defines the character of a river. Metamorphic and igneous rocks, which have greater resistance, look vastly different than softer sedimentary rocks. The rule here is: igneous rocks wear round and smooth; metamorphic rocks are jagged and plate-like; sedimentary rocks are crumbly. The Cache La Poudre is not geologically typical of front range rivers, thus the river is unlike any other river in Colorado.

The bedrock underlying most of the river is metamorphic rocks of Precambrian age. This basically means the rocks are hard and old. The original layers were laid down as clay and sand. These types of rocks are classified as sedimentary. As a mixture of flour, eggs, salt, and milk is heated and becomes a cake, comparatively sedimentary rocks get cooked into metamorphic rocks. The clays and sandstones (sedimentary rocks) were changed into schists (metamorphic rocks). These rocks are brittle and readily break into dish-plate-thick chunks.

Some rocks in the canyon have been forged from Earth's centrally located cauldrens. We see these as granites. The crystalline granites are classified as igneous rocks. Greyrock, Horsetooth Rock and Arthur's Rock are all examples of large granite formations that have pushed to the surface. In other places it pushes up in columnar fashion. The pallisades, near the Baldwin Tunnel, are a majestic example of these giants. Smaller trespassers sneak out in small bands. If you notice bands of lighter colored rocks pushing every which way in the darker rocks, you are seeing volcanic granite and quartz sneaking out of their inner earth cauldron.

The combination of these resistant rocks have created a V-shaped valley that is as narrow as 0.1 miles wide and up to 1,000 feet deep. The river flows through cobble and broken bedrock. Along the valley walls the soils are thin to non-existent. This produces sheer rock bluffs, bare rock ridges and ridge spines. The non-porous character of the rock causes precipitation to run directly into the stream and not into any ground-water reservoirs.

Lying 30 miles north of the "mineral belt," mining has been limited. Mining of gold, copper, uranium, mica and lead has yielded poor production levels. There is even a diamond mine in the vicinity. This commercial grade diamond mine was found in Chicken Park between the North Fork of the Poudre and the mainstem. The lack of mining in the area leaves the Poudre with no toxic tailings leeching into the river. This may be the only major drainage in Colorado that can make such a boast.

A unique geologic aberration can be seen starting at mile marker 86 and continuing up to the top of the canyon. The characteristic U-shaped canyon here was created by the downhill march of a glacier. The glacier ended its march at the Home Moraine. Here the leftovers of the digestion process were deposited into a huge pile. This site is called the Home Moraine site and has a little informative board for your reading pleasure. The river no longer is filled with broken bedrock but with gravel and glacial silt. The river also noticeably meanders and drops only half of its 63 feet per mile average. This is truly an interesting and unique geologic feature of this great river.

Originally a range of mountains west of our present mountains arose. Being hundreds of millions of years old when our present day Rockies were pushed up, they washed away and filled the area around Fort Collins with their alluvium. (Alluvium is not a dirty word. It is the cobble and sand left by a river. As the present day mountains rose, they to began to alluviate. (I made up that word.) Finally the present day Poudre Canyon was cut and its course set. A magnificent example of downward cutting on the Poudre is the Bellvue Dome or Goat Hill at the base of the canyon. Standing at Ted's Place and looking south, one cannot help but see a large facsimile of Moby Gym. Here the earth was lifted up and then covered over by the original mountains. Along came the Poudre and cut down through this dome, exposing a geologic anticline. This also was handy for the Native Americans to run buffalo off of in mass kills.

Looking from Ted's Place east, another geological occurrence is evident—the hogbacks of the front range are spectacular. In their book, *Cache La Poudre, The Natural History of a River,* Howard Ensign Evans and Mary Alice Evans say: "They are therefore tilted up toward the mountains, with more resistant strata forming the crests of the hogbacks, the more easily eroded forming the valleys." This is an excellent description of these beauties. If you head east, the first hogbacks you encounter are the oldest rock. The further you travel from the mountains, the younger the rocks become. Many amateur paleontologists (fossil hunters) know that the reddish layer, the Morrison Formation, yields evidence of inland oceans and large swamps in this area. The Western Interior Seaway extended from Alaska down to the Gulf of Mexico. The western shore extended into Montana, Wyoming, Colorado, and New Mexico. The eastern shore started in Minnesota and extended down to Oklahoma. All of the Gulf coast was submerged. The size of this ocean helps explain the discovery of fossils of large animals such as sharks teeth and giant turtle skeletons. The sea was the largest about 74 million years ago. Since then the ocean has been receding. Hopefully, the global warming will return the oceans to their old grandeur.

Getting Acquainted:
HABITAT OF THE AREA

The Cache La Poudre flows through five distinctly different habitats on its journey to Greeley. From the confluence with the South Platte in Greeley to Ted's Place is considered Plains. Most of the canyon is separated into Foothills and Montane Rocky Mountains. The head waters are a combination of Sub-alpine and Alpine Rocky Mountains. Below is a list of the most common types of plants to be found in each of the habitats.

PLAINS – Confluence with South Platte to Ted's Place

Sandlands	*Claylands*
sand bluegrass	bluegrass
sand dropseed	buffalo grass
little bluestem	western wheatgrass
needle and thread	dryland sage
prickly pear cactus	prickly pear cactus

FOOTHILLS/MONTANE – Eastern boundary of Roosevelt National Forest to Rustic

Foothills	*Pine Montane*	*Fir Montane*	*Aspen Montane*
wheat grass	sedges	spike fescue	sedges
blue stem	cinquefoil	chokecherry	yarrow
needleandthread	blue grama	serviceberry	pussytoes
mtn. mahogany	mtn. mahogany	douglas-fir	dandelion
ponderosa pine	ponderosa pine	poppies	aspen

SUB-ALPINE – Rustic to 2 miles above Spencer Heights

Lodgepole Pine	*Spruce Fir*
june grass	thurbur fescue
king fescue	bearded wheatgrass
sagebrush	kinnikinnik
pyrola	red raspberry
loco weed	canada buffalober
lupine	englemann spruce
lodgepole pine	subalpine fir

PIKA

Getting Acquainted:
ANIMAL SPECIES IN THE AREA

Key to the Abundance Notation (found to the right of each name)
AB–ABUNDANT   FC–FAIRLY COMMON   R–RARE   IRR–IRREGULAR
C–COMMON   U–UNUSUAL   END–ENDANGERED

Key to Seasonality Notation (found after slash)
Y – YEAR ROUND RESIDENT   W – WINTER RESIDENT
S-F – SPRING/FALL RESIDENT   SU – SUMMER RESIDENT
Example-Merlin (Falco culambaris)U/W: Merlin is uncommon and found in winter

List of Common and Scientific Names of Species
Found in the Cache La Poudre River Area

FISH

Sockeye Salmon/Kokanee(O. nerka)
Mountain Whitefish (Prosopium williamsoni)
Cutthroat trout (Salmo clarki)
Greenback Cutthroat Trout (S. c. stomias)
Rainbow Trout (S. gairdneri)
Brown Trout (Salvelinus fontanalis)
Fathead Minnow (Pimephales promelas)
Longnose Dace (Rhinichthys cataractae)
Creek Chub,northern (Semitolus atromaculatus atromaculatus)
Longnose sucker,western (Catostomus catostomus griseus)
White Sucker (C. commersoni)
Mountain Sucker (Pantusteus platyrhynchus)
Arctic Grayling (Thymallus arcticus)

AMPHIBIANS

Barred Tiger Salamander(Abystoma tiginum mavortium)C
Plains Spadefoot Toad (Spea bombifrons)C
Western Toad (Bufo boreas)FC
Woodhouse Toad ,Rocky Mountain (B. woohousei woodhousei)C
Striped Chorus Frog (Psuedacris nigrita maculta)C
Mountain Wood Frog (Rana sylvatica cantabrigensis)FC
Leopard Frog,western (R. pipiens brachycephala)C

REPTILES

Lesser Earless Lizard (Holbrookia maculata maculata)C
Red Lipped Rock Lizard (Sceloporus undulta erythrocheilus)C
Eastern Short-Horned Lizard (Phyrynosoma douglassi brevirostre)FC
Six-lined Racerunner (Cnemidorphus sexlineatus)C
Many-lined Skink (Eumeces multivirgatus multivirgatus)FC
Northern Water Snake (Natrix sipedon sipedon)FC
Wandering Garter Snake (Thamnophis elegans vagrans)C

Western Plains Garter Snake (T. radix haydeni)C
Red-sided Garter Snake (T. sirtalis parietalis)FC
Bull Snake (Pituophis catenifer sayi)FC
Prairie Rattlesnake (Crotalus viridis viridis)FC

*BIRDS

Common Loon (Gavia Immer)U/S-F
Arctic Loon (Gavia arctica)R/S-F
Western Grebe (Aechmorphus occidentalis)FC-AB/Y
Red-necked Grebe (Podiceps grisegena)R/S-F
Horned Grebe (P. auritus)FC-C/S-F
Eared Grebe (P. nigricollis)C-AB/S-F
Pied Billed Grebe (Podilymbus podiceps)FC/Y
Great Blue Heron (Ardea herodias)FC//Y
Black Crowned Night Heron (Nycticorax nycticorax)FC/S-F
Yellow-crowned Night Heron (Nyctanassa violacea)R/S-F
Snowy Egret (Leucophoyx thula)FC/S-F
American Bittern (Botaurus lentigenosus)U/S-F
Ross Goose (Chen rossii)R/W
Snow Goose (C. caerulescens)U/W
White Fronted Goose (Anser albifrons)R-U/W
Canada Goose (Branta canadensis)C-AB/Y
Brant (Branta bernicla)R/W
Mallard (Anas platyrhynchos)AB/Y
Gadwall (A. strepra)AB/Y
European Wigeon (Mareca penelope)R/S-F
American Wigeon (Mareca americana)AB/Y
Green-winged Teal (Anas carolinensis)AB/Y
Blue-winged Teal (A. discors)AB/W
Cinnamon Teal (A. cyanoptera)R-C/S-F
Northern Shoveler (Spatula clypeata)AB/Y
Pintail (Anas acuta)AB/Y
Redhead (Aythya americana)AB/Y
Canvasback (A. valisineria)C/S-F
Lesser Scaup (A. affinis)AB/S-F
Ring Necked Duck (A. collaris)FC-C/S-F
Common Goldeneye (Bucephala clangula)C/W
Barrows Goldeneye (Bucephala islandica)U/M
Bufflehead (B. albeola)C/S-F
Ruddy Duck (Oxyura jamaicensis)C-AB/S-F
Common Merganser (Mergus merganser)C/Y

Red-breasted Merganser (M. serrator)C//S-F
Hooded Merganser (Lophodytes cucullatus)U/S-F
Turkey Vulture (Cathartes aura)FC/Y
Marsh Hawk (Circus cyaneus)FC/Y
Sharped-shinned Hawk (Accipter cooperii)U-FC/Y
Goshawk (A. gentilis)U/Y
Red-tailed Hawk (Buteo jamaicensis)FC/Y
Swainsons Hawk (B. swainsoni)FC/S-F
Broad-winged Hawk (B. platypterus)R/S-F
Rough-legged Hawk (B. lagopus)C/W
Ferruginous Hawk (B. regalis)U/S-F
Golden Eagle (Aquila chrysaetos)FC/Y
Bald Eagle (Haliaeetus leucocephalus)U/Y
Gyrfalcon (Falco rusticolus)R/S-F
Prairie Falcon (Falco mexicanus)FC/Y
Peregrine Falcon (Falco pereginus)END/Y
Merlin (Falco columbarius)U/W
American Kestrel (Falco sparverius sparverius)FC-AB/Y
Blue Grouse (Dendragapus obscurus)FC/Y
White-tailed Ptarmigan (Lagopus leucurus)FC/Y
Merriams Turkey (Meleagris merriami)FC/Y
Virginia Rail (Rallus limocola)C/S-F
Sora (Porzana carolina)C//S-F
American Coot (Fulica americana)AB//Y
Black -bellied Plover (Squatarola squatarola)R-U/S-F
American Golden Plover (Pluvialis dominica)R/S-F
Killdeer (Charadrius vociferus)C/Y
Semipalmated Plover (C. semipalmatus)U-FC/S-F
Common Snipe (Capella gallinago)FC/S-F
Stilt Sandpiper (Micropalma himantopus)U-FC/S-F
Pectoral Sandpiper (Frolia melanotus)U/S-F
White-rumped Sandpiper (Erolia fuscicollis)R/S-F
Bairds Sandpiper (Erolia bairdii)FC-AB/S-F
Least Sandpiper (E. minutilla)C/S-F
Semipalmated Sandpiper (Ereunetes pusillus)FC-S-F
Western Sandpiper (Calidris mauri)FC/S-F
Solitary Sandpiper (Tringa solitaria)FC/S-F
Upland Plover (Bartamia longicauda)R-AB/S-F
Buff-breasted Sandpiper (Tryngites subrufficollis)R/S-F
Spotted Sandpiper (Actitis macularia)FC/S-F
Franklins Gull (Larus pipixcan)FC-AB/S-F
Foresters Tern (Sterna forsteri)U-FC/S-F
Black Tern (Chlidonias niger)U-FC/S-F
Band Tailed Pigeon (Columba fasciata)FC/S-F
Rock Dove (C. livia)C/S-F
Mourning Dove (Zenaidura macroura)AB/S-F
Long-eared Owl (Asio otus)U/Y
Skort-eared Owl (A. flammeus)U/Y
Great Horned Owl (Bubo virginianus)FC-C/Y
Screech Owl (Otus asio)U-FC/Y
Common Nighthawk (Chordeilus minor)AB/SU
Chimney Swift (Chatura palagica)U/SU
White-throated swift (Aeronautes saxatalia)U/SU
Broad-tailed Hummingbird (Selasphorus platycerus)FC/SU
Rufous Hummingbird (S. Rufous)FC/SU
Calliope Hummingbird (Stellula calliope)U-FC/SU
Belted Kingfisher (Megaceryle alcyon)FC/Y
Hairy Woodpecker (Picoides villosus)FC/Y
Downy Woodpecker (P. pubescens)FC/Y
Northern three-toed Woodpecker (P. tridactylus)U/W
Yellow-bellied Sapsucker (Sphyrapicus varius)R/SU
Williamsons Sapsucker (S. thyroideus)U/SU
Red-headed Woodpecker (Melanerpes erythrocephalus)R-U/SU
Lewis Woodpecker (M. lewis)U-FC/Y
Red-bellied Woodpecker (Centurus carolinus)R/Y
Common Flicker (Colaptes auratus)C/Y
Eastern Kingbird (Tyrrannus tyrannus)FC/SU
Western Kingbird (T. verticalis)C/SU
Cassins Kingbird (T. vociferans)U-FC/SU
Scissor-tailed Flycatcher (Muscivora forficata)R/SU
Olive-sided Flycatcher (Nuttallornis borealis)FC/SU
Western Flycatcher (Empidonax difficilis)R/SU
Traills Flycatcher (E. trailii)FC/SU
Least Flycatcher (E. minimus)U/SU
Hammonds Flycatcher (E. hamondii)FC/SU
Horned Lark (Eromophila alpestris)AB/Y
Cliff Swallow (Petrochelidon pyrrhonota)AB/SU
Barn Swallow (Hirunda rustica)AB/SU
Bank Swallow (Riparia riparia)U-FC/SU
Rough-winged Swallow (Steligidopteryx ruficollis)FC-C/SU
Blue Jay (Cyanocitta cristata)U/Y
Stellers Jay (C. stelleri)FC-C/Y
Scrub Jay (Aphelocoma coerulscens)FC/Y
Gray Jay (Perisoreus canadenis)FC/Y
Black-billed Magpie (Pica pica hudsonia)AB/Y
Common Raven (Corvus corax)FC/Y
Common Crow (C. brachyrhyncos)C-AB/Y
Clarks Nutcracker (Nucifraga columbiana)FC/Y
Pinyon Jay (Gymnorhinus cyanocephalus)FC/Y
Black-capped Chickadee (Parus atricapillus)FC-C/Y
Mountain Chickadee (Parus gambeli)FC/Y
Bushtit (Psaltriparus minimus)U/W
White-breasted Nuthatch (Sitta carolinus)U-FC/Y
Red-breasted Nuthatch (S. canadenis)U-C/Y
Pygmy Nuthatch (S. pygmea)FC/Y
Brown Creeper (Certhia familiaris)U-FC/Y
Dipper (Cinculus mexicanus)FC/Y
Rock Wren (Salpinctes obsoletes)U/Y
Canyon Wren (S. mexicanus)FC/SU
House Wren (Troglodytes aedon)C/SU
Winter Wren (T. troglodytes)R/W
Long-billed Marsh Wren (Telmatodytes palustris)U/S-F
Gray Catbird (Dumetella carolinensis)FC/SU
Brown Thrasher (Taxostoma rufum)R-FC/SU

Robin (Turdus migratorius)C/SU
Gray-cheeked Thrush (Hylocichla minima)R/S-F
Swainsons Thrush (H. ustuta)FC-AB/SU
Hermit Thrush (H. guttata)FC/SU
Varied Thrush (Ixoreus naevius)R/W
Eastern Bluebird (Sialia sialia)U/SU
Western Bluebird (S. mexicana)U-FC/SU
Mountain Bluebird (S. currucoides)C-AB/SU
Townsends Solitaire (Myadetes townsendi)FC/Y
Blue-gray Gnatcatcher (Polioptila caerulia)FC/SU
Golden-crowned Kinglet (Regulus satrapa)FC/Y
Ruby-crowned Kinglet (R. calenda)FC-C/Y
Bohemian Waxwing (Bombycilla garrulus)IRR/S-F
Cedar Waxwing (B. cendrorum)FC/S-F
Loggerhead Shrike (Lanius ludovicanus)U-FC/S-F
Starling (Starnus vulgaris)AB/Y
Red-eyed Vireo (Vireo olivaceus)R-U/SU
Philadelphia Vireo (V. philadelphicus)R/S-F
Warbling Vireo (V. gilvus)FC/SU
Solitary Vireo (V. solitaria)FC/SU
Bells Vireo (V. belli)R/SU
Yellow Warbler (Dendroica petechia)FC-C/SU
Yellow-breasted Chat (Icteria virens)U/SU
Wilsons Warbler (Wilsonia pusilla)C/SU
American Redstart (Setophaga ruticalla)R/SU
House Sparrow (Passer domesticus)AB/Y
Western Meadowlark (Sturnella neglecta)C/SU
Rufous-sided Towhee(Pipilo erythrophthalmus)FC/SU
Yellow-headed Blackbird (Xanthocephalus xanthocephalus)C-AB/SU
Red-winged Blackbird (Agelaius phoenicus)AB/SU
Evening Grosbeak (Hespiraphona vespertina)U-C/S-F
Pine Grosbeak (Pinicola enucleator)U-FC/Y
Blue Grosbeak (Guiraca caerulea)FC/Y
Cassins Finch (Carpodacus cassinii)FC/Y
Brown-capped Rosy Finch (Leucosteite australis)U-AB/Y
Common Redpole (Acanthis flammea)IRR/Y
Pine Siskin (Spinus pinus)U-FC/Y
Golden-crowned Sparrow (Zonotrichia atricapilla)R/W
Dark-eyed Junco (Junco nyemalis)FC-C/Y

*MAMMALS

Masked Shrew (Sorex cinereus)C
Wandering Shrew (S. vagrans obscurus)
Dwarf Shrew (S. nanus)U
Water Shrew (S. palustris navigator)FC
Merriams Shrew (S. merriami leucogenys)R
Pygmy Shrew (Microsorex hoyi monatanis)R
Least Shrew (Cryptotis parva parva)R
Little Brown Bat (Myotis lucifugus carissima)C
Long-eared Myotis (M. evotis evotis)R
Long-legged Myotis (M. volans interior)C
Small-footed Myotis (M. leibii)
Silver-haired Bat (Lasionysterus noctivagans)U
Big-brown Bat (Eptesicus fuscus pallidus)C

Hoary Bat (Lasiurus cinereus cinereus)FC
Townsends Big-eared Bat (Plecotus townsendi pallescens)C
Pika (Ochotona princeps)C
Eastern Cottontail (Sylvilagus floridanus)C
Nuttals Cottontail (S. nuttallii)C
Snowshoe Hare (Lepus americanus bairdii)C
Least Chipmunk (Eustamius minimus)C
Colorado Chipmunk (E. quadravittatus)C
Uinita Chipmunk (E. umbrinus montanus)C
Yellow-bellied Marmot (Marmota flaviventris)C
Richardsons Ground Squirrel (Spermophilius richardsoni elegans)C
Thirteen-lined Ground Squirrel (S. tridecimlinaetus)C
Rock Squirrel (S. variegatus grammurus)U
Golden-Mantle Ground Squirrel (S. lateralis)AB
Aberts Squirrel (Sciurus aberti)FC
Pine Squirrel (Tamiasciurus hudsonicus fremonti)C
Northern Pocket Gopher (Thomomys talpoides)C
Beaver (Castor canadensis concisor)C
Deer Mouse (Peromysus maniculatus)FC
Rock Mouse (P. difficulus nasutus)AB
Mexican Woodrat (Neotoma mexicana)C
Heather Vole (Phenacomys intermedius intermedius)U
Meadow Vole (Microtus pennsylvanicus)C
Montane Vole (M. montanus)AB
Long-tailed Vole (M. longicaudus longicaudus)C
Muskrat (Ondatra zibethicus)AB
Meadow Jumping Mouse (Zapus hudsonius preblei)R
Porcupine (Erithizon dorsatum)C-FC
Coyote (Canis latrans)C
Red Fox (Vulpe vulpes macroura)C
Swift Fox (V. velox velox)C
Gray Fox (Urocyon cinereoargenteus scotii)C
Racoon (Procyon lotor)C
Black Bear (Ursus americanus amblyceps)U-C
Marten (Martes americanus origenes)FC
Ermine (Mustela erminea muricus)U
Long-tailed Weasel (M.frenata)C
Mink (M. vison)FC
Badger (Taxidea taxus)FC
Spotted Skunk (Spilogale putorius)C
Striped Skunk (Mephitis mephitis)C
Mountain Lion (Felis concolor hippolestes)FC
Lynx (Lynx canadensis canadensis)END
Bobcat (L. rufus)C
River Otter (Lutra canadensis)END
Elk (Cervus canadensis nelsoni)C
Mule Deer (Odocoileus hemionus hemionus)C
White-tailed Deer (O. virginianus)C
Moose (Alces alces)R
Bighorn Sheep (Ovis canadensis canadensis)C-FC

KEY TO THE RIVER SECTION GUIDES

Each of the River Section Guides beginning on page 17 provides the following information.

SECTION NAME: Generally accepted name for that particular section of the river.

DIFFICULTY: Water level classification can be determined from the hydrograph on page 6. Class of water is determined from the International White Water Scale on page 6.

ABILITY: A general boater classification at medium water levels.
Beginner: Feels comfortable on Class I and II
Intermediate: Feels comfortable on Class III
Advanced: Feels comfortable on Class IV and V
Expert: Feels comfortable on Class VI

PUT-IN AND TAKE-OUT ELEVATION: Elevation gives a gauge of habitat and climate.

GRADIENT: Measured in the number of feet a run drops per mile.

TOPO MAP(S): USGS topographical map names

PUT-IN AND TAKE-OUT: Designated access for the prescribed runs. The actual accesses are infinite.

RIVER MILES: Number of river miles measured from put-in to take-out.

RIVER TIME: This is a subjective value to gauge time on the river at medium water level. Kayak time includes much play time. If you are kayaking straight through, use the rafting value.

MINIMUM AND OPTIMUM FLOW: Other subjective values to determine are the lowest and best runable level.

NUMBER: Mile markers are located on the south side of all roads and are a convenient reference point when driving the canyon.

NAME: Name of actual reference. Some poetic license was used because everyone has their own names. Your forgiveness is begged if your accepted name was not used.

SECTION TABLE: Found at the beginning of each chapter.

MAP: Maps are not proportional or to scale. They are designed to help locate references in relation to the road or other points in the book.

DISCLAIMER: *River running is an inherently dangerous sport. If you do not realize this, I recommend you stay home. There is no possible way for any guide to cover all of the obstacles. This publication is designed to give a general character to the river and to give points of reference. The rule is: When in doubt, SCOUT. This rule definitely applies to all experiences on the Cache La Poudre River.*

MAP OF THE POUDRE RIVER

How to find the Poudre

The runs described in this book are in the Poudre Canyon near Ft. Collins, CO. From I-25, take Hwy 14 west into Ft. Collins. Follow the signs for Hwy 14 & 287. Make a diagonal right turn onto Riverside. Next, turn right on College Ave., which is Hwy 287. Take Hwy 14 & 287 toward Laramie, WY. Turn left at Hwy 14 (Conoco station), which is signed as Poudre Canyon.

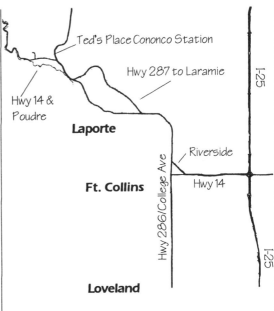

Ted's Place Cononco Station

Hwy 287 to Laramie

I-25

Hwy 14 & Poudre

Laporte

Riverside

Ft. Collins

Hwy 14

Hwy 286/College Ave

I-25

Loveland

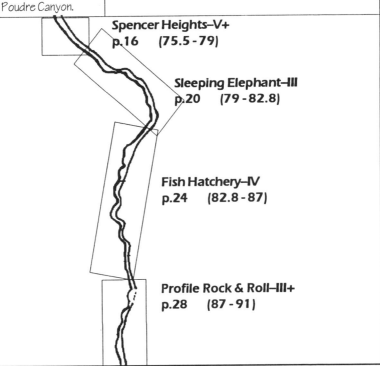

Spencer Heights–V+
p.16   (75.5 - 79)

Sleeping Elephant–III
p.20   (79 - 82.8)

Fish Hatchery–IV
p.24   (82.8 - 87)

Profile Rock & Roll–III+
p.28   (87 - 91)

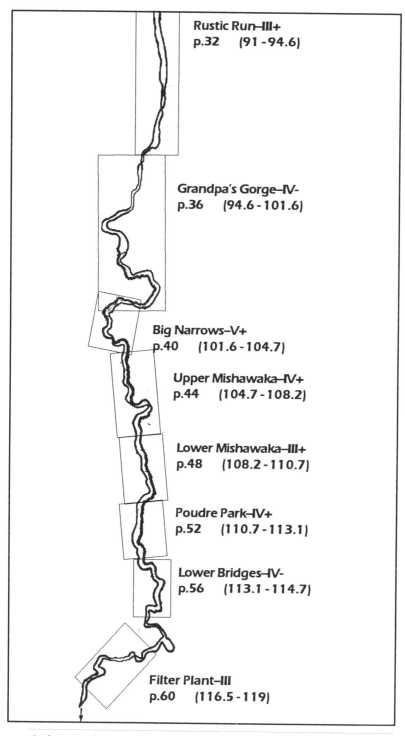

Rustic Run–III+
p.32   (91 - 94.6)

Grandpa's Gorge–IV-
p.36   (94.6 - 101.6)

Big Narrows–V+
p.40   (101.6 - 104.7)

Upper Mishawaka–IV+
p.44   (104.7 - 108.2)

Lower Mishawaka–III+
p.48   (108.2 - 110.7)

Poudre Park–IV+
p.52   (110.7 - 113.1)

Lower Bridges–IV-
p.56   (113.1 - 114.7)

Filter Plant–III
p.60   (116.5 - 119)

Spencer Heights—75.5 to 79

75.5 Kiehl Bridge put-in

75.6 Boneyard or Meatgrinder–V+

76.6 Tunnel Picnic Area

78.2 Spencer Heights Resort

78.4 Spencer Heights Bridge

78.5 Brown's Trading Post

78.6 Sportsman's Lodge

79 Sleeping Elephant take-out

Sleeping Elephant Campground

River Section 1. **SPENCER HEIGHTS**

Difficulty:	High: Class V+
	Medium: Class V
	Low: Class VI
Ability:	Expert / Advanced
River miles:	3.5 miles
River time:	Kayak–3 hours; Raft–Possible with one mandatory portage

Put-in (8,218'):	Just past bridge on north side of road
Take-out (7,820'):	Across street from Sleeping Elephant campground USFS camping picnic ground
Minimum flow:	500 cfs
Optimum flow:	2,000 cfs
Gradient:	119 feet per mile
Topo map:	Boston Peak, CO

The Spencer Heights Run is best described by the word "change." Starting as a Class V+ and dropping to a Class II meander, this is an excellent run on a diverse alpine river.

75.5 Kiehl Bridge

The put-in for this run is upstream of the bridge. Very steep and rocky.

75.6 Boneyard or Meat Grinder

Either name is appropriate. This run is filled with multiple broach and vertical pin situations. The crux of this rapid is connecting a slot that begins river left and ends river right but has no connecting slot. After the pool, a milder but still class V+ rapid develops in a narrow canyon.

76.6 Tunnel Picnic Area

The river changes from a tiger to a rabbit and becomes a Class III with lots of play spots and "time-to-read" rapids. This picnic ground is a great spot for rafters and intermediate-level kayakers to jump in. One of the best spin holes on the river can be found here. This picnic ground marks a stop for a stage that ran from Walden to Fort Collins in 1880-1881. The stage changed horses here and serviced silver mining boom towns Lulu City and Teller City.

76.7 Laramie-Poudre Tunnel

Completed in 1906, this was one of the first water projects in the West. The tunnel is 9 feet tall and 2-1/4 miles long. Water is piped from the Laramie River and deposited in the Poudre. Someone believed that irrigating the plains near Greeley was more important than the grasslands of southern Wyoming. This probably was not the ranchers of southern Wyoming.

78.2 Spencer Heights Resort

78.4 Spencer Heights Bridge

The land here is heavily posted and trespassing is definitely discouraged. The final 3/4 of a mile is relatively uneventful for white water, but just past Spencer Heights Resort is a very low bridge. This should be scouted for clearance and possibly portaged. The land above the bridge on river left is public and can be used for landing and scouting.

78.5 Brown's Trading Post

78.6 Sportsman's Lodge

79 Sleeping Elephant Mountain

This distinct landmark is directly across from a large campground. Exiting here is very convenient. The take-out is on the left side of a long island, and parking is across the street.

79 Sleeping Elephant Campground

YELLOW-BELLIED MARMOT

Photo by Amy Maddox

River Section 1. **SPENCER HEIGHTS**

Sleeping Elephant—79 to 82.8

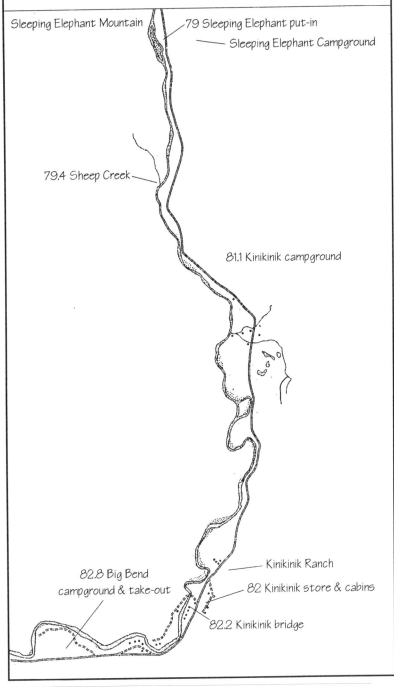

Sleeping Elephant Mountain

79 Sleeping Elephant put-in

Sleeping Elephant Campground

79.4 Sheep Creek

81.1 Kinikinik campground

82.8 Big Bend campground & take-out

Kinikinik Ranch

82 Kinikinik store & cabins

82.2 Kinikinik bridge

Difficulty:	High: Class III
	Medium: Class II+
	Low: Class III-
Ability:	Intermediate
River miles:	5.0 miles
River time:	Kayak–3 hours; Raft–2 hours

Put-in (7,820'):	Across the street from Sleeping Elephant campground
Take-out (7,740'):	Big Bend Picnic area USFS picnic
Minimum flow:	500 cfs
Optimum flow:	2,000 cfs
Gradient:	30 feet per mile
Topo maps:	Kinnikinik, CO & Boston Peak, CO

While there are many reasons to call the Poudre "wild," this section of the river is not one of them. This fits the "scenic" definition much better. The alpine habitat and the distance from the road can give those with an active imagination a trip down an Alaskan glacial river. The two pre-run precautions pertain to river temperature (very cold) and trees (many lie dead in the river).

79 Sleeping Elephant Mountain

79 Sleeping Elephant Campground

This marks the put-in. Across the highway behind a fence is a fire access road. Park in the campground and walk over to the river

79.4 Sheep Creek

This creek flows from atop Sleeping Elephant Mountain out of the Commanche Wilderness Area. Much of the south side of the river is within this wilderness area.

80 Mount Wanderer (9,866') and Boston Peak (9,363')

In the spring a wonderful waterfall flows between these two mountains.

81.1 Kinnikinik Campground

On river left a newer facility can be used for lunch and potty breaks. (You'd never guess I have a toddler.)

82 Kinnikinik Ranch

The large open meadow on the north side of the road marks this ranch. Built in 1867 by an Englishman named Blackmer, it is said to be the oldest standing building in the canyon. Many Englishmen came to America to settle and raise cattle. They were referred to as remittance men because of the money sent to them from home. Being of lesser nobility or younger sons, they were entitled to no land from inheritance. Therefore, they got along like present-day college students: "*Mom and Dad, please send money. I need a ranch.*" *Signed, Spoiled English Gentry*

82 Raven's Rook

A local landmark found on river right, this large hunk of granite is named for the obvious profile.

82 Owl Rock

River right reveals a likeness to this infamous nighttime hunter

82 Kinnikinik Store and Cabins

This historic site appears on river left. This would be the oldest resort up the canyon, if it were open. A short aside on Kinnikinik: Besides being fun to type and say, a kinnikinik is a low, waxy-looking shrub. Derived from an Indian name, it can be spelled many different ways. Indians would pound the kinnikinik berries into vennison to make pemmican. This was the preferred way to eat the berries since the berries taste

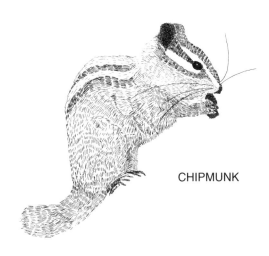

CHIPMUNK

atrocious. Dried and used in teas, or smoked, the leaves have a mildly intoxicating effect. They must be combined, however, with tobacco and willow bark to attain the narcotic effect. The most important aspect of kinnikinik is the source of food it provides for animals during the winter.

82.2 Kinnikinik Bridge

Here, the first true obstacle spans the river. A bridge with a center pylon keeps you against the left bank.

82.8 Big Bend Campground

The bathrooms and picnic tables on river left mark your departure point. Be sure to eye the meadows north of the road, for this is prime bighorn sheep country. Spring brings the Division of Wildlife out with matches to "improve" this habitat for "wildlife." The future may bring a bighorn sheep observation area. Soon you may be able to sit in your car and experience wilderness.

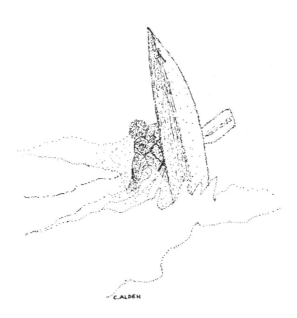

C.ALDEN

Fish Hatchery—82.8 to 87

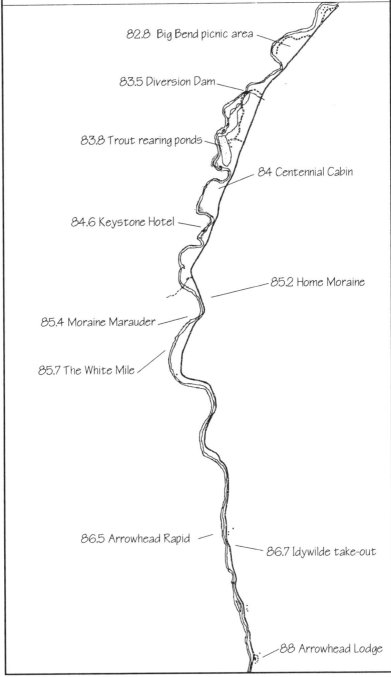

82.8 Big Bend picnic area

83.5 Diversion Dam

83.8 Trout rearing ponds

84 Centennial Cabin

84.6 Keystone Hotel

85.2 Home Moraine

85.4 Moraine Marauder

85.7 The White Mile

86.5 Arrowhead Rapid

86.7 Idywilde take-out

88 Arrowhead Lodge

River Section 3. **FISH HATCHERY**

Difficulty:	High: Class IV
	Medium: Class III+
	Low: Class III
Ability:	Advanced
River miles:	5.5 miles
River time:	Kayak–4 hours; Raft–2 hours

Put-in (7,740'):	Big Bend Picnic area USFS picnic
Take-out (7,400'):	.5 miles above Arrowhead Lodge
Minimum flow:	250 cfs
Optimum flow:	2,000 cfs
Gradient:	58 feet per mile
Topo maps:	Rustic, CO and Kinnikinik, CO

This is a schizophrenic, "wild and scenic" river run. Beginning as a glacial valley where the river meanders gently and ending as an advanced set of tight, technical drops, this run gives a smorgasbord of what the Poudre has to offer. Change characterizes the Poudre, and this section has plenty. Presently, few boaters run this stretch.

82.8 Big Bend Picnic Area

This alpine put-in has the usual aspen, pines and firs. It is difficult to find a more picturesque point in the Poudre canyon. While you are drifting out of the put-in and being lulled into a serene stupor, try to remember that ahead lies a Class VI "play spot."

83.5 Diversion Dam

Pass under a center pylon bridge and move to river left with great haste. This structure is in the river to divert water into a Division of Wildlife facility. The act of portaging to some is an admission of great cowardice. I prefer to think of it as a heroic act of discretion, especially in the face of a keeper/killer hydraulic. A road runs next to the left bank of the river, and a nice re-entry point is just downstream of the diversion dam. Below the dam a series of chain link fences extend into the river about 20 feet from either shore.

83.8 Poudre Trout Rearing Ponds

This facility can be seen during the next mile on river left.

83.9 Beaver Swimming Hole

As the river begins a left turn, a stupendous swimming hole beckons the brave and cold-blooded. Beware of large rodents in the water. This is the domain of several beaver families. These large, flat-tailed rodents attracted the original European explorers to the Poudre Canyon. The beaver's fur has sharp barbs on the longer guard hairs, which can be persuaded to intertwine and create a tightly "woven" material that was in great demand in the 1700s and 1800s for stylish top hats. Many of the early explorers were French, which is evident in many of the local names: LaPorte, Platte, Laramie and the Cache La Poudre. When rafting and kayaking along the territories of these benign dam builders, watch for sharp submerged sticks. Beavers stash these in deep pools to have the bark available for winter food. If greeted by a beaver's sharp tail slap, you have formally been asked to cease your trespassing.

83.9 Meanders

On river left two diversions return the water they "borrowed" from above. The greatest obstacles along these twisting hairpins are the anglers. I call them anglers because they do not kill fish. These fly fisherman try to think and feel like a fish. They try to imitate the trouts' food source and to fool one into a brief social encounter. *(Limit your kill. Don't kill your limit.)*

84 The Centennial Cabin

This cabin was used in the filming of the movie "Centennial." The book *Centennial,* written by James Mitchner, accurately documents the history of this area.

84.6 Keystone Hotel

On the right side of the river lies the site of this historic cabin. Built in 1896 by Mike and John Zimmerman, it was three stories high, had forty rooms, and slept 100 people. Rooms ranged from $8 to the outlandish cost of $14 a night. In 1946 the notorious Fish and Game Department bought and disassembled this landmark.

85.2 The Home Moraine

A moraine is defined as "deposits left on the side and end of a glacier." When the glacier ended its march in the Poudre Canyon it left a deposit directly in the path of the Poudre River. The glacier passed through many different types of rocks, which can be observed here. There is evidence of at least three glacial advances. Approximately 8,000 years ago, a global warming trend melted the glaciers. Since then the earth has gone through a cooling period until fifty years ago when the earth began a gradual warming.

85.3 Twin Peaks

Two large boulders span the river and create two channels. Be especially careful of deadfall in this section. Below, look for two magnificent waves for pounding in a raft or surfing in a kayak.

85.4 Moraine Marauder

This is a Class III rapid with a large hole in the center and a second hole on river left. High water makes these ugly.

85.7 The White Mile

Fast, technical, big waves, big holes, and no eddies make this a run to cherish. A roadside or riverbank scout will show few rocks but there are some major holes to avoid. Be extra wary of the hole near the end on river right. It likes to eat boaters. Class IV rapid.

86.5 Arrowhead Rapid

A fun Class III rapid delivers you to a small road and a pleasant take-out.

88 Arrowhead Lodge

MAGPIE

Profile Rock—87 to 91

87 Idywilde put-in —

87.2 Arrowhead Island —

88 Arrowhead Lodge —

88.3 Profile Rock —

88.8 Old Poudre City & Stamp Mill —

89 Chapel Bridge III —

91 Rustic Resort & Old Water
Wheel House take-out —

River Section 4. PROFILE ROCK & ROLL

Difficulty:	High: Class III+
	Medium: Class III
	Low: Class III-
Ability:	Intermediate
River miles:	4.0 miles
River time:	Kayak–2.5 hours; Raft–1.5 hours

Put-in (7,400'):	.5 miles upstream of Arrowhead Lodge
Take-out (7,160'):	Rustic Resort
Minimum flow:	250 cfs
Optimum flow:	2,000 cfs
Gradient:	68 feet per mile
Topo map:	Rustic, CO and Kinnikinik, CO

This stretch of river is usually an add-on to the Fish Hatchery Run or the Rustic Run. The scenery is mired in private homes and the shortness makes it not worthwhile for a day trip. The majority of the run is Class II/III- but one Class III+ does limit this run to very solid intermediates.

88 Arrowhead Lodge

This property was acquired by the United States Forest Service through a land exchange deal. The Forest Service uses this as an information center and has a person on scene to assist poor lost souls. Drop in, say "hi" and see how the new-generation Forest Service is beginning to seriously consider the recreator as a resource.

87 Idywilde

The put-in lies across from a small community of houses.

87.2 Arrowhead Island

An island can divert you either direction, yet kayakers may desire the left channel for its spectacular surfing.

88.3 Profile Rock

While passing the island, be sure to look up and notice the geological formation on river right. It is an excellent example of the two types of rock found in the canyon. The forehead is formed from igneous (granite) rocks and weathers into smooth rounded corners. Thus the rounded forehead. The metamorphic rocks weather into jagged blocks and plates, which forms the nose and chin. These rules can be applied anywhere in the canyon to identify the rock types.

88.8 Old Poudre City

On June 10, 1891, the Poudre ran at its highest ever flow. Exceeding the recorded 21,000 cfs, the river roared down the Poudre Canyon. One fatality is the town on your left. This mining community of 50 people came about due to the rumor of gold. These people's dreams of riches were washed away with this massive flood. No real gold strikes were ever found in the canyon.

88.8 Stamp Mill

A testimonial to the mining era is the chimney from this gold processing mill that can be seen on river left.

89 Chapel Bridge

Here is a good place to scout. Underneath the bridge is a cross-cut rock that forms a ledge hole across the entire river. This could prove to be hazardous at certain levels. On the other hand, I have seen kayakers playing here for hours. III

89.5 Poudre River Resort

89.8 Mountain Greenery

90.5 Bighorn Cabins

91 Glen Echo Resort

90.9 Scorched Tree Bed and Breakfast

91 Rustic Resort

Rustic is a user-friendly take-out, and by simply talking to the owners you can get permission and directions to the designated take-out.

91 Old Water Wheel House

A left-hand run around an island brings you to a large bank with a dilapidated old building that is the old electric generator for the Rustic Resort. This is the take-out and is a Class V exit. Be careful.

EASTERN COTTONTAIL

River Section 5. **RUSTIC RUN**

Rustic Run—91 to 94.6

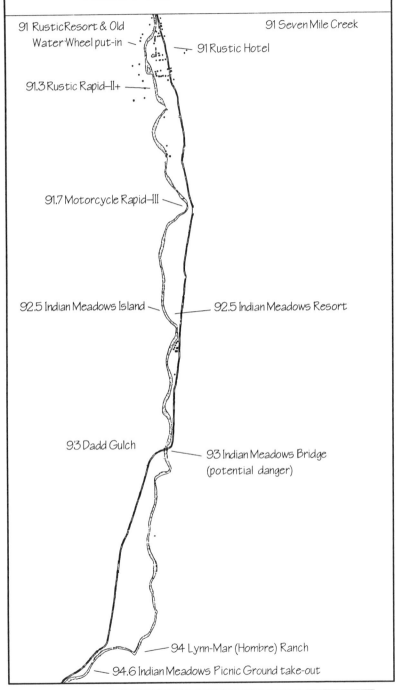

91 RusticResort & Old Water·Wheel put-in

91 Seven Mile Creek

91 Rustic Hotel

91.3 Rustic Rapid–II+

91.7 Motorcycle Rapid–III

92.5 Indian Meadows Island

92.5 Indian Meadows Resort

9.3 Dadd Gulch

93 Indian Meadows Bridge (potential danger)

94 Lynn-Mar (Hombre) Ranch

94.6 Indian Meadows Picnic Ground take-out

River Section 5. **RUSTIC RUN**

Difficulty:	High: Class III+
	Medium: Class III
	Low: Class III-
Ability:	Intermediate
River miles:	5.0 miles
River time:	Kayak–2.5 hours; Raft–1 hours

Put-in (7,160'):	Rustic Resort
Take-out (6,998'):	.5 miles above Grandpa's Bridge USFS picnic area
Minimum flow:	250 cfs
Optimum flow:	2,000 cfs
Gradient:	32 feet per mile
Topo maps:	Big Narrows, CO & Rustic, CO

The Rustic Run is very popular among intermediate boaters who wish to escape the masses on the Bridges Run. The run is extremely scenic and has some good whitewater. Runable longer than the other upper stretches, it becomes too bony by about 2.5 on the rock. The water runs fairly fast but is unobstructed. A must for all intermediates.

91 Rustic Resort

Put-in is behind the resort on private property. By asking these kind people for permission, you will meet some extraordinary individuals.

91 Old Water Wheel

The put-in is the original site for a power generating water wheel. A wooden flume brought water past the resort to supply energy for this area long before the modern lines brought electricity to Rustic.

91 Rustic Hotel

Built in 1881 by S.B. Stewart, this hotel reportedly housed Teddy Roosevelt during one of his outings.

91 Seven Mile Creek

Great little mountain biking and hiking trail. Follow Seven Mile Road up and to the left on 4-WD road.

91.3 Rustic Rapid

A Class II+ rapid with nice waves and a great exit eddy. There is a split rock just beyond which creates a powerful hydraulic. Avoid this if you are of intermediate level or less.

91.7 Motorcycle Rapid

Drinking and driving can be detrimental to yourself, others and your insurance rates. When a person drinks too much, gets on his/her motorcycle, and then drives off the road into the Poudre, we get a great rapid name. I don't know how accurate this story is, but it sure sounds great. Keep to river left through rock gardens. The river begins to bend right at the entrance to Motorcycle Rapid. Notice the 40-foot drop from the road to the river, and imagine the delight as you fly free and unhindered. Imagine the feeling as you land. The fall doesn't hurt. It's the sudden stop that gets you. A Class III rapid.

92.5 Indian Meadows Resort
92.5 Indian Meadows Island

Both forks are runnable at high water, but at lower water take the hard right-hand fork. Many Indian artifacts and actual teepee rings from past inhabitants on Indian Meadows Island can still be found. The Arapahoe, Cheyenne and Utes all considered this their territory at one time or another. Now, it is privately owned. Please ask permission from the resort before landing on this island.

BIGHORN SHEEP

93 Indian Meadows Bridge

For many, decapitation is a great way to remove 10 pounds of ugly fat. If this is not your idea of a weight-loss plan, check to see the level of the river as it runs under this bridge. This bridge was re-built in 1990 to take out two major curves in the highway. You may get out on either side of the river to check the clearance. It has been my experience that "3" on the rock is not enough space.

94 Lynn-Mar (Hombre) Ranch

This land was purchased by the USFS and gives access to a great stretch of river. The metamorphic rock has also made numerous cavities in the rock. Watch for small gray birds here. They are almost comical as they stand by the water bobbing and diving into the rapids to nab insects off the rock. The river ouzel, or dipper, nests in these cavities and feeds along this stretch. The nests are usually built on an overhanging rock out of grasses and mosses.

93 Dadd Gulch

A hiking trail rises to the south and meets the Crown Point Road. Excellent mountain biking and hiking. Large fields of blueberries and raspberries.

94 .4 Boy Scout Corner

Boy Scout Corner? you ask. The quick and painless story says a group of Boy Scouts were stranded here and consequently rescued. A Class II rapid.

94.6 Indian Meadows Picnic Ground

A USFS picnic ground on river right bank. You have found your take-out.

River Section 6. **GRANDPA'S GORGE**

Grandpa's Gorge—94.6 to 101.6

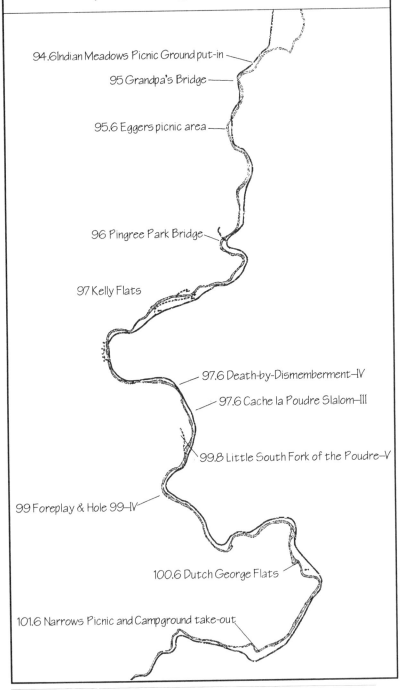

94.6 Indian Meadows Picnic Ground put-in

95 Grandpa's Bridge

95.6 Eggers picnic area

96 Pingree Park Bridge

97 Kelly Flats

97.6 Death-by-Dismemberment—IV

97.6 Cache la Poudre Slalom—III

99.8 Little South Fork of the Poudre—V

99 Foreplay & Hole 99—IV

100.6 Dutch George Flats

101.6 Narrows Picnic and Campground take-out

River Section 6. **GRANDPA'S GORGE**

Difficulty:	High: Class IV- Medium: Class III+ Low: Class IV-
Ability:	Advanced / Intermediate
River miles:	8 miles
River time:	Kayak–4.5 hours; Raft–2.5 hours

Put-in (6,998'):	.5 miles above Grandpa's Bridge USFS picnic area
Take-out (6,487'):	Narrows Campground USFS camping and picnic
Minimum flow:	300 cfs
Optimum flow:	2,500 cfs
Gradient:	43 feet per mile
Topo maps:	Big Narrows, CO and Rustic, CO

Late May through late June, Grandpa's Gorge portrays the wild and scenic character for which this river is notable. High to medium high water makes this run a wild series of cataracs and scenic pools. At low water, a rock jumble is frustrating and dangerous. Even though the river runs next to the road, the river runner is presented with the illusion of being completely isolated. This run becomes more and more popular each year. The rules are: make an early season run, wear protection (neoprene not latex), and be aware of the multitudes of islands.

94.6 The Indian Meadows USFS Picnic Ground

A put-in that has several tables and a fantastic eddy. There is a nice warm-up stretch to prepare shoulders or crews. By the time the bend is rounded, the river constricts and begins to pick up speed.

95 Grandpa's Bridge

Grandpa's Gorge begins here. It is a Class IV- rapid that is tight and powerful.

95.6 Eggers USFS Picnic and Fishing Facility

The fishing and scenery along this stretch are fantastic.

96 Eggers or Pingree Park Bridge

County Road 63E leads up toward Pingree Park and the Little South Fork of the Poudre. Other accessible points from this road are: Crown Point, Pennock Pass, Buckhorn Canyon, and Masonville. Several campgounds exist up this road, as do miles of mountain biking.

97 Kelly Flats Campground

Kelly Flats was named after an old trapper, Jim Kelly, who frequented these parts and was hired as a wild-meat hunter for workers in the canyon. He eventually was run off for procuring cows instead of elk.

97.6 Foo-Fang Falls or Death-by-Dismemberment

The scout for this drop is identifiable by either spotting Bennett Creek on river right or by sighting the foot bridge. Get out on river left, which gives you the road to walk and a better angle for entering the falls. What you see is worse visually than it is hydraulically. There is a six-foot drop that ends in a large rooster tail. Enter the rapid from the left and push through to the right. Rafters need to warn crew members sitting on the left to watch their heads as they pass a large block of concrete that hangs down from the bridge. This is a good place to set in-laws, bosses and obnoxious neighbors as the left-side crew. "Honestly, officer, I had no idea they would stand up as we passed under the bridge."(Forgive me a cruel chuckle, HA) The preceding has been a joke of the National Sarcasm Association. Once again, this was only a joke. Really! A calm pool leaves time for high fives. A Class III+ rapid.

97.6 Cache La Poudre Slalom

The location of this old race makes for a fun-filled Class III rapid. Kayakers, be aware of the multitude of surfing spots.

98.8 Mountain Park Campground

Directly in front of the campground either left or right channels can be taken. Avoid the exceptionally sharp rocks against the right bank. Kayakers – look for the great side-surfing holes just before the bridge. The bridge is a signal for a scouting outing.

99 Foreplay and Hole 99 (Double Drop)

Foreplay is a Class IV rapid with plenty of drama potential. Use the short break between Foreplay and Hole 99 to regain your composure. Hole 99 always seems to supply some excitement. The double drop design of the hole makes it trickier than it appears. The far right run is clean and leads you into some hidden razor rocks that can, and have, ripped rafts and kayaks. Scout closely and choose carefully.

99.8 Little South Fork of the Poudre

This tributary comes in on river right. This fork is divided into both "wild" and "recreational" under the National Wild and Scenic designation. This run begins up County Road 63E and is not covered in this edition. A beautiful and intense stretch, it is for experts only. This is one of only two stretches of the Cache La Poudre that has "wild" status under the designation. The remoteness and inaccessability make this Class IV/V Section more like a Class V/VI.

100.6 Dutch George Flats

Sitting at the confluence of the Poudre and Elkhorn Creek, this was the home of a trapper-hunter named (would you ever guess) Dutch George. Recognized as an archaeological site, the old cabin, trash pit, and fruit trees can be seen near the creek. Artifacts and bones can be dug from the trash site. The legend says that Old Dutch George protected his trapping area with great enthusiasm and ironically shot himself with his own rifle while skinning a bear.

101.6 Narrows Picnic and Campground

In front of the picnic ground are two excellent waves that will keep you entertained indefinitely. Be sure to take-out here unless you are ready for disembowlment or other such fun hobbies. The Big Narrows lies ahead.

Rafters enjoy Death by Dismemberment on the Grandpa's Gorge run. Photo courtesy of Rocky Mountain Adventures.

Big Narrows—101.6 to 104.7

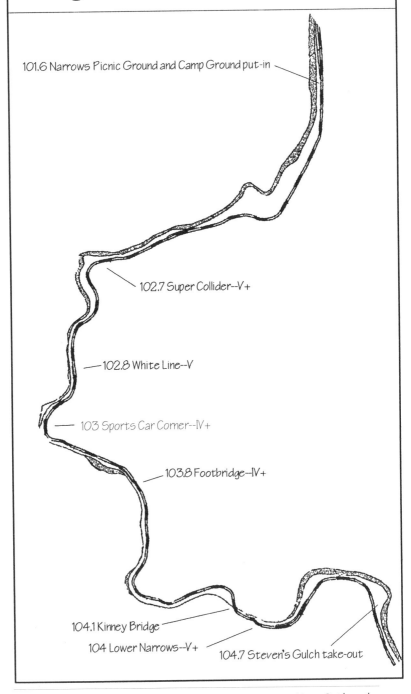

101.6 Narrows Picnic Ground and Camp Ground put-in

102.7 Super Collider--V+

102.8 White Line--V

103 Sports Car Corner--IV+

103.8 Footbridge--IV+

104.1 Kinney Bridge

104 Lower Narrows--V+

104.7 Steven's Gulch take-out

River Section 7. **BIG NARROWS**

Difficulty:	High: Class V+
	Medium: Class V
	Low: Class V-
Ability:	Expert
River miles:	4.0 miles
River time:	Kayak–4.5 hours; Raft–not recommended

Put-in (6,487'):	Narrows campground USFS camping and picnic
Take-out (6,080'):	Stove Prairie landing USFS camping/picnic
Minimum flow:	200 cfs
Optimum flow:	500 cfs
Gradient:	102 feet per mile
Topo map:	Big Narrows, CO

The narrows can be broken into three distinct runs. The first is the Upper Narrows, which is big and powerful. Second is the Middle Narrows, which is much slower and playful. Finally, is the Lower Narrows, which is technical and steep. Many now run this stretch.

101.6 Narrows Picnic Ground and Campground

This is the put-in for the Upper Narrows. The first quarter of a mile down from the picnic ground is relatively easy.

102.7 Super Collider

The drop on the corner is a potential pin spot and is regularly portaged even by hair boaters. The narrowing becomes most obvious below, as it becomes a torrential 200+-foot-per-mile drop. All of this water moves through a mere 20-foot-wide gap. After scouting this for two or more hours, it only takes seconds to run. The portage is on river left near a culvert. V+

102.8 White Line

This rapid has been run at nearly every level and warrants great respect. Large holes and huge volumes of water make this a precision run. Class V+ rapid.

103 Sports Car Corner

Both a put-in and rapid, this signals the beginning of the Middle Narrows. A Class IV+ run with tight and technical rapids.

103.8 Foot Bridge

A significant drop with pin potential. The foot bridge marks the beginning of a fantastic Class IV+ rapid.

104.1 Kinney Bridge

Wonderful spin hole just above here. Take-out for the middle narrows and put-in for the lower narrows (classV+). This run can be scouted from the road. At low water be aware of the nasty sharp rocks. At high water, the hydraulics are powerful and sticky.

104.7 Steven's Gulch

After the river slows down, a developed picnic ground is a nice take-out.

105 Upper Landing

A developed boat facility used by all of the commercial companies.

105.4 Stove Prairie Landing

Whether boating The Narrows or just gawking, it is a great geological lesson. The rock throughout this stretch weathers by becoming rounded and smooth. It is also resistant to weathering and erosion and is narrower than the stretches above and below it. These characteristics suggest igneous granite, which is the predominant rock in this section.

Entering second drop of the Lower Narrows.

Gary Brunner enters the Lower Narrows.

Upper Mishawaka—104.7 to 108.2

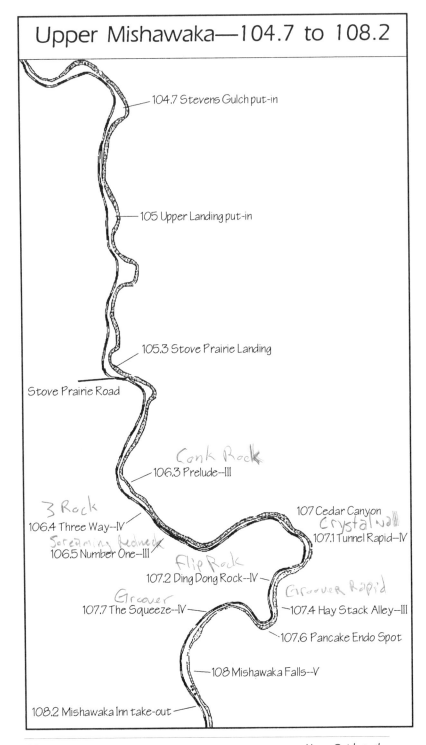

104.7 Stevens Gulch put-in

105 Upper Landing put-in

105.3 Stove Prairie Landing

Stove Prairie Road

Conk Rock

106.3 Prelude–III

3 Rock

106.4 Three Way--IV

Screaming Redneck

106.5 Number One–III

107 Cedar Canyon

Crystal wall

107.1 Tunnel Rapid–IV

Flip Rock

107.2 Ding Dong Rock--IV

Groover Rapid

Groover

107.7 The Squeeze--IV

107.4 Hay Stack Alley--III

107.6 Pancake Endo Spot

108 Mishawaka Falls--V

108.2 Mishawaka Inn take-out

River Section 8. **UPPER MISHAWAKA**

Difficulty:	High: Class IV+
	Medium: Class IV
	Low: Class III+
Ability:	Advanced
River miles:	2.9 miles
River time:	Kayak–2 hours; Raft–45 minutes

Put-in (6,080'):	Stove Prairie Landing USFS camping/picnic
Take-out (5,871'):	Mishawaka Inn
Minimum flow:	350 cfs
Optimum flow:	2,000 cfs
Gradient:	70 feet per mile
Topo maps:	Poudre Park, CO and Big Narrows, CO

The Upper Mishawaka run is a classic western run. Big water in a narrow river makes the fun fast and furious. Big waves and big holes are de rigeur. Across the river to the north, Red Mountain rises to an elevation of 7,464 feet. The river noticeably narrows in this stretch, which suggests harder or more resistant rock. An increase in the amount of quartz in the rock can be observed by the tannish-pink outcrops.

104.7 Steven's Gulch

This USFS campground has boat launching facilities.

105 Upper Landing Rest Area

An alternate put-in when Steven's Gulch is crowded.

105.3 Stove Prairie Landing USFS

This picnic and campground serves as an overnight spot and picnic ground, but boat launching from this area will no longer be permitted because of user conflicts.

106.3 Prelude

A semi-technical run that should be entered on river left to miss a major pour-over. You'll find this rapid as you round a blind left-hand turn. A Class III rapid.

106.4 Three Way

One way to run this is to skim along the left wall, move right of a large hole, slide left into the slot, catch the back eddy, and finally move between two large rocks. Joseph Campbell said, "The conquest of fear yields the courage of life." Mark Campbell said, "Who is that stupid son of a bitch getting tagged in the hole." To paraphrase and combine: Enjoy this rapid, but scout it first. A Class IV rapid.

106.5 Number One

Named for its likeness to the Classic Numbers Run on the Arkansas, this one is great fun. One step easier and much shorter, it only deserves Number One designation. Rafters can do some power paddling through these waves and get some spectacular soakings. Kayakers begin the surfing safari. A Class III rapid.

106.8 Sandbag Corner

In 1983 the Poudre escaped its usual parameters and wandered out onto the road. Let us pray for more of these years.

107 Cedar Canyon

A side hike here is highly recommended. On river left, where no good eddy exists, a canyon leads off to the northwest. After landing and tying up your boat, hike toward the canyon entrance. There is lots of cactus here to threaten your feet. The canyon is narrow, deep and shady. Therefore, it is very lush and humid. Follow the marginal path up the canyon and you will see an old mine off to your right. This man-made cave goes back only 30 feet or so and poses no danger. Farther up, you will be surrounded by huge pillars with falcon nests, waterfalls, spring peepers, and a plethora of plants. This is called The Palisades. These granite intrusions are truly beautiful geologic specimens. When the hot magma within the earth needs to strike forth into the world, it pushes up through other types of rocks and is seen as streaks of white, orange or pink. These are called "dikes" when they are perpendicular to the surrounding rock and "sills" when they are parallel to surrounding rock formations.

107.1 Tunnel Rapid

This Class IV+ rapid is named for the historic tunnel just downstream. Scout from river right. Be extra careful of the pin wall at the end. Non-bailing rafts are highly discouraged here because the water load created by the holes make the pull away from the pin wall difficult at best. Kayakers—don't depend too much on the cushion wave at the bottom. This pin wall is under cut. A Class IV rapid.

107.2 Baldwin Tunnel

This historic tunnel was built in 1916 and was the final link between the lower Poudre Canyon Road and the road from Cameron to Rustic.

107.4 Ding Dong Rock or USS (ultimate squirt spot)

This Class IV rapid sits on a left-hand corner. Preceding Ding Dong Rock are three holes that force an S-turn manuever that leaves you near enough to the rock to ring its doorbell.

107.5 Hay Stack Alley

A series of Class III standing waves. Kayakers can surf some of these, but there are better play spots below.

107.6 Pancake Endo Spot

As you come around the large right-hand bend, notice the flat rock on river left. In a kayak, at certain water levels, the endo spot will slap you like a pancake on the rock. At different levels the endo spot becomes a keeper hole. At certain levels, however, this will put you vertical and aerial. Be careful at high water levels and low water levels.

107.7 The Squeeze

A 4- to 5-foot wave at medium water, this wave gives kayakers a good chest thump and stands a raft up on end. High water (above "4" on the rock) can flip a raft.

108 Mishawaka Falls

A stretch of rock dodges and holes alerts one to the most technical rapid on this stretch. A Class IV+ rapid to be taken seriously. Pull your boat off to river right and scout this one carefully.

108.2 Mishawaka Inn

On weekends, park your boat on the river behind the Inn, listen to the free live music from your boat, and beg beers from the patrons. The take-out is just beyond the Inn on river right. Once again, check with the management for any special requirements. This is private property.

Lower Mishawka—108.2 to 110.7

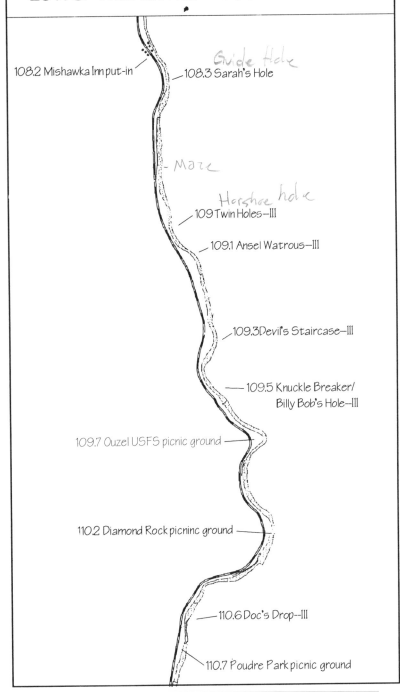

108.2 Mishawka Inn put-in

Guide Hole

108.3 Sarah's Hole

- Maze

Horshoe hole

109 Twin Holes—III

109.1 Ansel Watrous—III

109.3 Devil's Staircase—III

109.5 Knuckle Breaker/ Billy Bob's Hole—III

109.7 Ouzel USFS picnic ground

110.2 Diamond Rock picninc ground

110.6 Doc's Drop--III

110.7 Poudre Park picnic ground

River Section 9. LOWER MISHAWAKA

Difficulty:	High: Class III+
	Medium: Class III
	Low: Class III-
Ability:	Intermediate
River miles:	3.2 miles
River time:	Kayak–2 hours; Raft–45 minutes

Put-in (5,871'):	Mishawaka Inn
Take-out (5,720'):	Poudre Park picnic area USFS picnic
Minimum flow:	300 cfs
Optimum flow:	2,000 cfs
Gradient:	50 feet per mile
Topo map:	Poudre Park, CO

An intermediate run that has many play spots. This run is the final run that is totally within the National Wild and Scenic designation. Below here, the possibility and probability of a dam is very scary.

108.2 Mishawaka Inn

This is the original site of Walter Thompson's homestead. Built in 1916, this became the lower Poudre's first resort. This is also the point where the Poudre Canyon highway ended until 1919. Previously, travelers would be detoured to Livermore, west toward Redfeather, and then down to Rustic. The road then proceeded over Cameron Pass to Walden. Now, Mishawaka Inn is a river access and a fine dining establishment. Before you put in here, check with the management for any special requirements. This is private property and can be avoided by putting in downstream 100 yards. In the past, owners have requested a signed liability waiver and payment of one dollar to use their property. Be sure to respect their wishes.

108.3 Sarah's Hole

This is a large hole that has very grabby edges. Kayaks can skirt this hole on river left, but rafters need to hit this one at ramming speed. On the ridge on river left is a good place to see bighorn sheep. Near the top, an old burn provides perfect big horn habitat. Look for the sheep moving early in the morning. Later in the day, they might be sighted lying on a rocky outcrop. Sheep, which once were plains animals, are easily stressed. Both sexes have horns but males' curl over and can exceed a full curl.

109 Twin Holes

As "twin holes" suggests, there are two. Rafters at full speed can splash the back of the boat with a sumptuous lick from the first hole. Kayakers who are prepared and skilled can find nirvana in the first hole. An elevator ride up and down, with beer foam in your armpits, lets you know the true meaning of life. Both rafters and kayakers beware of the next hole. The surge pulls up on the rock and those unprepared or unskilled can flip or wrap here.

109.1 Ansel Waterous

USFS camp and picnic ground slips by off to river right as you navigate a Class III rock garden.

109.3 Devils Staircase

A rock garden with many raft rippers and broach spots found 100 yards down stream of Ansel Waterous. A Class III+ rapid.

109.5 Knuckle Breaker / Billy Bob's Hole

A Class III rapid with a keeper hole near the bottom left. The two holes following Knuckle Breaker make nice aprés-rapid splashes.

109.7 Ouzel USFS Picnic Ground

Keep a good grip on your valuables as you lurch over the final drop. It is a bit bumpy.

110.2 Diamond Rock

USFS camp and picnic spot. Watch out for anglers trying to catch more of those federally fed fish-hatchery welfare fish. Diamond Rock is the large piece of granite on river left, across from a rock covered with "tourons" with fishing poles and red coffee cans full of worms.

110.6 Doc's Drop or Doctor Suckhole

A four-foot drop lies just above the parking, picnic, and take-out spot. This is another advisable scout. The sneak run is on far river left. A chute exists just left of the hole and another exists right of the hole. Do not run the hole. It is a boat eater. A Class III rapid.

110.7 Poudre Park Picnic Ground

Take-out, picnic tables and bathrooms are here.

Rafters on the Mishawaka Run. Photo courtesy of Rocky Mountain Adventures.

Poudre Park—110.7 to 113.1

110.7 Poudre Park Picnic Ground put-in

111.3 Hewlit Gulch Bridge *Shut the Hell up Bridge*

112 Poudre Park Slalom Course--III

112.1 Fountain Rock

Bridge

112.1 Decapitation Bridge–II

112.3 Nail Bridge–III

112.2 Bolt Bridge--III

112.3 Cardiac Corner--IV

PineVu Hotel Remains

112.4 The Golf Course–III

112.7 River Gauge

112.7 PineVu Falls–IV

Pine Box

112.9 Nine Rock Rapids--III

113.1 Poison Ivy Corner take-out

River Section 10. POUDRE PARK

Difficulty:	High: Class IV+
	Medium: Class IV
	Low: Class IV-
Ability:	Advanced
River miles:	2.8 miles
River time:	Kayak–2 hours; Raft–45 minutes
Put-in (5,720'):	Poudre Park USFS picnic
Take-out (5,518'):	1 mile east of Poudre Park on large bend
Minimum flow:	300 cfs
Optimum flow:	2,000 cfs
Gradient:	69 feet per mile
Topo map:	Poudre Park, CO

For advanced and enthusiastic intermediates, this is the graduate run from the Lower Bridges run. At medium water a minimum of six Class IV rapids exist. Five bridges must also be negotiated. Both the scenery and the gradient increase in intensity from the Lower Bridges run, which makes this an exciting and challenging advanced run.

110.7 Poudre Park Picnic Ground

The put-in has toilets, tables, and plenty of parking.

111.3 Hewlett Gulch Trail

If you are inclined to mountain biking, this is a great trail. More importantly, this bridge marks the beginning of the stretch of river designated as "recreational" under the National Wild and Scenic River system. From this point upstream for 38 miles of the mainstem, no major river diversions or buildings can be built. Kayakers will find an endo spot under the bridge here on river right. At medium levels, expect a flyswatter ender. At high water, be careful not to get maytagged in the hydraulic. Be wary of some old bridge pilings down river 50 yards. These are potential raft rippers.

112 The Poudre Park Slalom Course

This is one to be avoided by rafts in low water. It becomes a dragging marathon and is not pretty. Medium to high water leaves multitudes of channels.

112.1 Fountain Rock

In a kayak this little ski jump drops both your boat and your heart as you shoot through the 2-foot-wide gap. Be sure there is no flotsam wedged before you try. It really does no good to know this after you have tried. Directly after Fountain Rock is the second bridge.

112. 1 Decapitation Bridge

Decap is so named for a bar that deceptively lies at neck level. As you go under the bridge a wave lifts you to the Decap level, and a timely "duck" command from the raft captain is welcomed and needed for all crew members, unless your mother-in-law, creditor or other undesirable is on board.

112.2 Bolt Bridge

At the base of the bridge piling is a strategically located bolt. This bolt is legend to have a hypalon and tupperware magnet. Stay center in the wave train and easily avoid the bolt. Kayakers will find a very surfable wave above Bolt Bridge.

HUMMINGBIRD

112.3 Nail Bridge

Scouting this rapids from solid ground is highly recommended. On river right, an old lodge with cabins can be seen and is a perfect landing site for scouting. Do you wonder why the name Nail Bridge? Well, the thoughtful people who built this bridge figured it might be nice to add nails throughout the cement and bend all of their sharp ends up stream. So, as you approach Nail Bridge a crowd of upstream-pointing nails greets your boat or flesh. The point being, do not touch the walls as you pass through your chosen channel.

112.3 Cardiac Corner

In mid-June this is a fine flower-viewing spot. The large orange blossoms with black centers are poppys. The blooming of the poppys is an accurate dating mechanism for peak run-off. There is usually a large number of taller purple flowers. These are mountain flax, and they bloom most of the summer. Cardiac at high water is a screaming right-hand turn with an ugly whirlpool and pin rock combo. At low water, it is a technical drop through jagged rocks and a whirlpool with a pin rock. *Don't underestimate Cardiac.* A Class IV rapid.

112.4 The Golf Course

Rafters are frequently heard screaming in a post-cardiac adrenaline state as they plow through these excellent waves. Kayakers should stop for an endo spot when the road is back in sight on river right. A Class III+ rapid.

112.7 Pineview Falls

On river right a landing and eddy is evident. Use this spot as a scouting stop. Pineview Falls may well be the "best" rapid on the Poudre. A Class IV rapid.

112.7 River Gauge

The rock on river left just above Pineview Falls has numbers painted in fluorescent orange. Everyone refers to the rock level instead of cfs.

112.9 Nine Rock Rapid

At high water several holes exist, and at low water it is an ugly rock garden with pin-and-press spots galore. A Class III+ rapid.

113.1 Poison Ivy Corner

Here is the take-out for this stretch and the beginning of Lower Bridges.

Lower Bridges—113.1 to 114.7

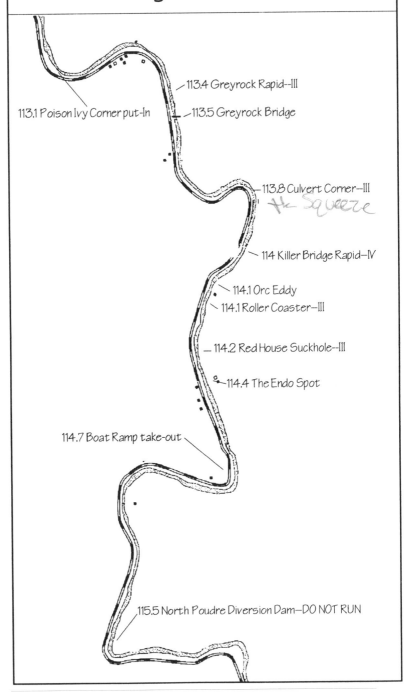

113.1 Poison Ivy Corner put-In

113.4 Greyrock Rapid--III

113.5 Greyrock Bridge

113.8 Culvert Corner--III

the Squeeze

114 Killer Bridge Rapid--IV

114.1 Orc Eddy

114.1 Roller Coaster--III

114.2 Red House Suckhole--III

114.4 The Endo Spot

114.7 Boat Ramp take-out

115.5 North Poudre Diversion Dam—DO NOT RUN

Difficulty:	High: Class IV-
	Medium: Class IV
	Low: Class III+
Ability:	Advanced / Intermediate
River miles:	3.0 miles
River time:	Kayak–2 hours; Raft–45 minutes

Put-in (5,518'):	1 mile east of Poudre Park in parking lot on large bend
Take-out (5,420'):	Just above North Poudre Diversion Dam
Minimum flow:	200 cfs
Optimum flow:	2,500 cfs
Gradient:	33 feet per mile
Topo map:	Poudre Park, CO

This is probably the most popular run on the Poudre – and for good reason. A moderate run with many play spots, it has propelled to classic status.

113.1 Poison Ivy Corner

The epitome of skin afflictions can be readily identified by its shiny three-leafed branches. The first exposure is usually a non-irritant. Subsequent exposures lead to an ugly rash that irritates like taxes. The put-in is a semi-maintained USFS area. Many commercial companies use this improved road shoulder and they appreciate it if you unload next to the river and then move your car up-river to the parking area. This saves the bus drivers much aggravation as they try to unload their precious cargo of fortuitous floating funseekers.

113.4 Greyrock Rapid / Bridge

The only precaution here is a ledge hole two-thirds of the way down the rapid. Greyrock Bridge is a clear landmark. The center pylon divides the river near center. Kayakers would be well-advised to eddy behind the left pylon and to jump into the surf wave downstream of the center pylon. The Greyrock Bridge connects the parking on the opposite side of the road to a 2-1/2 mile trail to the bottom of Greyrock Mountain. This is an easily accessed take-out or put-in. Greyrock Mountain is another excellent example of igneous rock that has been exposed through weathering. A Class III rapid.

113.8 ~~Culvert Corner~~ Squeze

Underneath the large culvert a large ominous-looking wave gnashes its teeth. This wave is not as nasty as it first appears. In a raft, it is merely a splasher. In a kayak it is a fun surf and potential endo spot.

114.0 Killer Bridge Rapid

This rapid is the crux of the run. Killer Bridge is a pushy Class IV rapid at high water and a boulder-choked set of Class III drops at low water. A large eddy above the rapid on river left gives you an opportunity to scout the upcoming rapid. Once again be aware of the poison ivy. At the bridge, most people run left of the central pylon – but use your own best judgment.

114.1 Orc Eddy

Orc Eddy is named for the souls who successfully run Killer in a kayak. They owe the river orc an eskimo roll. A silly river superstition to appease the river gods. I always do two.

Rafters safely negotiate Greyrock Bridge. Photo courtesy of Rocky Mountain Adventurers.

114.1 Roller Coaster

A Class III rapid that consists of a series of large-standing waves that thump kayakers and soak rafters. Low-water hazards include a nasty sleeper mid-rapid on river right and a nasty hole on river left.

114.2 Red House Suckhole

Red House, at high water, is a keeper/killer hole when run incorrectly. Kayakers will revel and roll in the fantastic hole downstream from Red House.

114.4 The Endo Spot

An excellent "grin" spot that can be backed up with 10 to 12 kayaks when it is working just right on a weekend. When the river hits "4" on the rock, the endo spot seems to work best.

114.7 Boat Ramp

This a very popular take-out. Be considerate when parking. Great surfing in Legend Hole.

115.5 The North Poudre Diversion Dam

The dam was built in the 1950s as part of the Colorado-Big Thompson project. Water is diverted into the north Poudre irrigation ditch. This is the end of Bridges Run and should not be run at any level. High water creates a keeper hydraulic. Low water produces a meat grinder of rocks. From here down to the Filter Plant Run is taboo. The Water Works has put up fences and some huge killer diversions. **Do Not Run.**

KINGFISHER

Filter Plant—116.5 to 119

116.5 Filter plant put-in

117.1 Big Bend--III

117.6 Gypsy Terrace B&B
117.6 Hole in the Wall Bridge

117.5 Sluice Box--II

117.9 Maddog--III

118 Water Battle Alley

118.6 Indian Gulch

118.8 360 Rapid--II

119 Picnic Rock State Park Take Out

120.4 Diversion Dam to Monroe Gravity Canal--DANGER

River Section 12. FILTER PLANT

Difficulty:	High: Class III
	Medium: Class II+
	Low: Class II
Ability:	Beginner / Intermediate
River miles:	2.9 miles
River time:	Kayak–2.5 hours; Raft–1 hour

Put-in (5,360'):	.3 miles east of Filter Plant across from Householder's home
Take-out (5,278'):	Picnic Rock S.P. picnic area
Minimum flow:	250 cfs
Optimum flow:	2,000 cfs
Gradient:	30 feet per mile
Topo map:	LaPorte, CO

The Filter Plant Run is the stretch many new boaters run on their first river outing. This run is classified as a "beginner-intermediate" run. This is to imply that rudimentary skills should be in place. These should include: basic strokes and braces, wet exit, eddy turns, and good white-water floating technique. My theory is you must swim 100 miles or get competent instruction before you are classified as a competent river runner, and I decided to swim my 50 miles on this stretch. Also, do not underestimate this stretch for its great surfing.

116.5 Fort Collins Water Treatment Plant

The put-in for the Filter Plant Run is within sight of the water treatment plant at the end of the Householder driveway. On the north side of the river you will find a wide area and a sloping drive that leads down to the river. This is for unloading only. Do not park here or you might find your car as the new filter plant surfing wave. Across the street on the south side, you will see a large clearing for parking. Do not park in front of Mr. Householder's drive. This is his driveway, and it is rude to block his access.

117.1 Big Bend, Turkey Corner or Kamikazee Corner

The second name refers to the number of neophytes who swim this rapid. The rapid contains several haystack waves that combine with several transverse waves, and is a perfect spot to practice your braces or pull away rowing techniques. Directly below Big Bend on river left is a nice eddy for rescues or attempts to paddle back into Big Bend's squirrely waves. A Class II+ rapid.

117.5 Sluice Box

Sluice Box is an exciting set of waves leading into a huge pool with super squirrely eddy lines. Many a kayaker has been given the opportunity to practice his/her roll here, and many a rafter has been given the opportunity to practice the whitewater float position in this "pool." A Class II rapid.

117.6 Hole in the Wall Bridge

There are no pilings to worry about under this bridge and the run is fun and clear for the next 100 yards. As you pass under the bridge, try to look up and see the cliff swallows. Through the end of June you can catch glimpses of the fledglings sticking their heads out of their penthouses. Below the bridge on river right you will encounter an exquisite wave.

117.6 Gypsy Terrace Bed and Breakfast

117.9 Maddog Rapid

The entrance to this right-hand-turn rapid is a nice calm pool. The best line begins to the right of Maddog rock. Maddog rock is a large rock that is a major river divider at low water and an ugly pour-over at high water. After passing just right of Maddog rock the current will carry you toward the left bank through some standing waves. As soon as you get past these waves you should begin to work toward river right. A Class III rapid.

118 Water Battle Alley

Rafters have been known to acquire a taste for world domination as they try to drown even their closest friends in other boats. Thus the name. On river left, the bank is covered with wild plums. In the spring the fragrance is one of the greatest in nature. In early fall the fruit is spectacularly tart.

118.6 Indian Gulch

The river runs flat and straight to a ninety degree bend to the left. At the top of this bend is a large eddy on river right. A park and hike from here is a trip into another ecosystem. From the beach, follow the gulch up past several pools and meadows. The gulch flows year around and is extremely lush. There are chokecherry bushes, Indian rice, raspberries, alder, dogwood, plum, mint, and many wildflowers (July). This is a nice place for lunch or an afternoon stroll.

118.8 360° Rapid

Many commercial companies try to see how many 360-degree rotations they can make in the length of this rapid. Now, try to remember that most commercial customers are poor souls from other countries, such as Kansas or Illinois. Some are even from Third World countries such as New Jersey. A Class II rapid.

119 Picnic Rock State Park

Take-out along here, for below looms certain doom – a very dangerous diversion dam.

120.4 Diversion Dam to Munroe Gravity Canal

At high water it is a keeper/killer hydraulic. At low water it is a food processor waiting to process all who venture here. Below this point the river is criss-crossed with barbwire and cut and drained by various diversion dams. Therefore, this book will not cover it. ***Here Be Dragons.***

121.7 Ted's Place

122 KOA Campground

MERGANSER

Rafters at Doc's Drop on the Lower Mishawake 9 Run. Photo courtesy of Rocky Mountain Adventures.

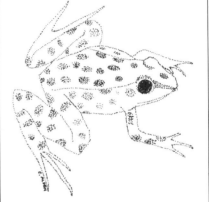

Author Bryan Maddox surfing at Legend Hole.

PICNIC AREAS & CAMPGROUNDS

Poudre Park

Mile Marker Location: 111
Use(s):   Picnic
Overnight Fee: Not applicable
Number of Sites: 2
Amenities: Toilet   Y
                          Water   N
                          Trash   N

Description: Here, the put-in for the Upper Bridges run and the take-out for the Lower Mishawaka run make this a busy picnic ground. A shuttle parking spot is provided upstream from the toilet and picnic tables. Doc's Drop is a fun little Class III drop, where one can usually see a good thrashing or two.

Diamond Rock

Mile Marker Location: 110.5
Use(s):   Picnic
Overnight Fee: Not applicable
Number of Sites: 10
Amenities: Toilet   Y
                          Water   N
                          Trash   N

Description: Right next to the river at an elevation of 5,747 feet, is a beautiful picnic ground that beckons the fisherman, kayaker, rafter and any other river rat type. Look directly north across the river and you can see the diamond-shaped rock for which this picnic ground was named.

Ouzel

Mile Marker Location: 110
Use(s):   Picnic, Fish
Overnight Fee: Not applicable
Number of Sites: 4
Amenities: Toilet   Y
                          Water   N
                          Trash   N

Description: Can be used as a take-out or put-in.

Ansel Watrous

Mile Marker Location: 109
Use(s): Camping
Overnight Fee: $7/night; electrical hookups more
Number of Sites: 22
Amenities: Toilet   Y
                Water   Y
                Trash   Y

Description: Ansel Watrous is the largest campground below the Narrows. Contiguous to the Lower Mishawaka run, this campground always seems to have a few cars with kayaks or rafts attached. Named for an editor for the *Fort Collins Courier*, circa 1911.

Stove Prairie

Mile Marker Location: 105.5
Use(s): Camping
Overnight Fee: $7/night per site
Number of Sites: 12
Amenities: Toilet   Y
                Water   N
                Trash   N

Description: Another busy spot, many boaters have discovered this run and this spot has seen overcrowding from time to time. Try not to walk through the unimproved campsites to get to the river. This disturbs some campers.

Upper Landing

Mile Marker Location: 105
Use(s): Picnic, boat ramp
Overnight Fee: Not applicable
Number of Sites: 6
Amenities: Toilet   Y
                Water   N
                Trash   N

Description: If pull-out is full, try one of the other three access points for this run.

Stevens Gulch

Mile Marker Location: 104.5
Use(s):   Picnic, boat ramp
Overnight Fee: Not applicable
Number of Sites: 6
Amenities:

Toilet	Y
Water	N
Trash	N

Description: Just before the Narrows, a small road with a gate crosses a shallow stem of the Poudre River. After crossing this mighty torrent, a small but rarely crowded parking area appears. With a large calm eddy and a series of nice waves and holes, this is my personal choice for the Upper Mishawaka run. Stevens Gulch can be seen northwest of the put-in and, when accessible, is a nice hike. Look for additional parking on the south side of the road.

Narrows Picnic Ground

Mile Marker Location: 102
Use(s):   Picnic, boat
Overnight Fee: Not applicable
Number of Sites: 14
Amenities:

Toilet	Y
Water	N
Trash	N

Description: The Narrows Picnic Ground is connected to the Narrows Campground. This is the preferred take-out for the Grandpa's Gorge run. If you have just run Grandpa's Gorge, this is a good spot to know – below is the Narrows. If you are putting in, may the force be with you.

Narrows Campground

Mile Marker Location: 101.5
Use(s):   Camp
Overnight Fee: $7/night per site
Number of Sites: 12
Amenities:

Toilet	Y
Water	Y
Trash	Y

Description: Surrounded by cottonwoods and pines, this campground divides the river nearly in half from Filter Plant to Laramie-Poudre Diversion Tunnel. There is also access to hiking and mountain biking trails.

Dutch George Flats

Mile Marker Location: 100.5
Use(s): Camping
Overnight Fee: $7.00
Number of Sites: 25
Amenities: Toilet Y
Water Y
Trash Y

Description: Upstream along the road there is a pair of dips. These double dips signal a great hiking and biking trail. This trail leaves the road going north up a well-marked gulch.

Century Park

Mile Marker Location: 100
Use(s): Picnic
Overnight Fee: Not applicable
Number of Sites: 3
Amenities: Toilet Y
Water N
Trash N

Mountain Park

Mile Marker Location: 99
Use(s): Picnic, camping, RV
Overnight Fee: $7/night per site
Number of Sites: 52
Amenities: Toilet Y
Water Y
Trash Y

Description: Having the river between you and the road creates a sound buffer for this campground. During the summer on weekends expect a full campground. Arrive early or use the USFS reservation system.

Kelly Flats

Mile Marker Location: 97
Use(s): Camping
Overnight Fee: $7/night per site
Number of Sites: 38
Amenities: Toilet Y
Water Y
Trash Y

Description: Jimmy Kelly lived in this area in the 1890s. He was the meat provider for the building of the skyline ditch. After a local rancher was missing some of his slow elk (cows), Jimmy was "asked" to leave the valley.

Eggers

Mile Marker Location: 95.5
Use(s):   Fishing
Overnight Fee: Not applicable
Number of Sites: Not applicable
Amenities: Toilet   Y
                           Water   N
                           Trash   N

Description: Eggers was an old settlement that consisted of a school-house, chapel and the Poudre City Stamp Mill used for processing ore. In 1891 it was destroyed when the Chambers Lake Dam broke.

Indian Meadows

Mile Marker Location: 92.5
Use(s):   Picnic, Fishing
Overnight Fee: Not applicable
Number of Sites: 2
Amenities: Toilet   Y
                           Water   N
                           Trash   N

Description: Located at the west end of Hombre Ranch, this picnic site is a rare treat. The wild trout water has plenty of trout, and the hills to the north are year-round habitat for deer, elk and a herd of bighorn sheep. Whether rafting, kayaking or picnicing, take time to walk along this riparian habitat.

Big Bend

Mile Marker Location: 83
Use(s):   Camping
Overnight Fee: $7/night per site
Number of Sites: 9
Amenities: Toilet   Y
                           Water   Y
                           Trash   Y

Description: Soon to be a big horn sheep observation area, this spot is a beauty. Typical U-shaped glacial valley with prime bighorn habitat, this is the best upper canyon stop. Be sure to check the fishing regulations.

DIPPER

PICNIC AREAS & CAMPGROUNDS

Sleeping Elephant

Mile Marker Location: 79
Use(s):   Camping
Overnight Fee: $7/night per site
Number of Sites: 19
Amenities: Toilet   Y
                         Water   Y
                         Trash   Y

Description: Look west and then east and you now know what a classic glacial valley looks like. Now, look south and observe the immense rock that bears the carved of this campsite. High within the sub-alpine zone, you'll see many aspen, spruce and fir trees. Across the road, a fire access for attaining water is easily identified. Do not block this access, but it makes a fine put-in/take-out.

Tunnel

Mile Marker Location: 77
Use(s):   Picnic, boat
Overnight Fee: Not applicable
Number of Sites: 4
Amenities: Toilet   Y
                         Water   N
                         Trash   N

Description: The old site of the construction city for Laramie-Poudre Tunnel project. This city had bunkhouses, a commissary, and a small hospital. The electricity came from a water wheel near the Poudre Falls.

Colorado State Park Picnic Rock

Mile Marker Location: 119
Use(s):   Picnic, boat
Overnight Fee: $3/per vehicle per day or annual State Parks Pass ($30)
Number of Sites: 12
Amenities: Toilet   Y
                         Water   Y
                         Trash   Y

Description: Picnic Rock has two parts. The upper area has covered tables and grills. The lower area has picnic tables and a shack for the ranger. Great source for river information or emergencies.

RESORTS

Fort Collins KOA

PO BOX 600, Bellvue, CO. 80512
(970) 493-9758

Facilities: Camping, rustic cabins, RV hookups, bathroom, showers, phone
Services: Convenience store, water, RV dump
Description: Located east of US 287 at the base of the Poudre Canyon. KOA offers several ways to overnight, including camping on individual plots beginning at $14; rustic cabins at a starting price of $25; and for those of a RV persuasion, prairie schooners can receive full hookups for a nominal fee.

Conoco Oil Inc.

92 Poudre Canyon Rd., Bellvue, CO 80512
(970) 493-2676

Facilities: Phone
Services: Convenience store, fresh donuts, coffee, gas, water, air
Description: Previously known as Ted's Place, this establishment is noted on most maps. Ted's Place marks the beginning of the great Poudre Canyon. This is a great place for stocking up on munchies, gasoline, drinks and any other little necessities.

Gypsy Terrace Bed and Breakfast

4167 Poudre Canyon Hwy., Bellvue, CO 80512
(970) 224-9389

Facilities: Two non-adjoining rooms
Services: Private bath, large living room, wood-burning stove, redwood deck, full breakfast
Description: Four miles up the canyon from Ted's Place is a bed and breakfast that once was a rowdy dance hall and saloon. In the 1930s the Gypsy Terrace was not known for its private rooms and exceptional breakfast. (It was known by a more social reputation.) At $60 for a double and $55 for a single, this is an excellent lower Poudre bargain.

Mishawaka Inn

13714 Poudre Canyon Hwy., Bellvue, CO 80512
(970) 482-4420

Facilities: Camping, bathroom, showers, phone
Services: Restaurant, live music, ampitheater, bar
Description: Located 13.7 miles from the junction of Hwy 14 and 287, the Mishawaka has been around since 1916. As a put-in, better check with the

management for a possible waiver. As an entertainment center, Mishwaka seems to get better every year. Providing live music on Friday, Saturday and Sunday, this river establishment makes for a great pre- or post-trip stop.

Rustic Resort

31443 Poudre Canyon, Bellvue, CO 80512
(970) 881-2179

Facilities: Camping, RV parking, rustic cabins, modern cabins, showers, phone

Services: Restaurant, convenience store, bar, liquor store, gas, water

Description: Rustic Resort is on the map. This resort used to be on the stage line that served the mining communities of Lulu City and Teller City. This historic site features both the Old Rustic Hotel (built in 1881) and the site of the first electricity generating water wheel. Located near mile marker 91, the Rustic Resort offers boaters both overnight facilities and a put-in. The camping is $6 and up. There are rustic and modern cabins starting at $30. If you would like to use this as your put-in or take-out, the owners request only a signed waiver releasing them from the infamous liability. This is an excellent put-in and take-out.

Glen Echo Resort

31503 Poudre Canyon Hwy., Bellvue, CO 80512
(970) 881-2208 or 1-800-348-2208

Facilities: Rustic cabins, modern cabins, full baths, fireplaces, RV hookups, showers, restrooms, phone

Services: Groceries, convenience store, large gift shop, restaurant, gasoline, propane, water, free wildlife museum

Description: Glen Echo is under the oldest ownership of any establishment in the canyon. Purchased in 1957, Glen Echo is the department store of the canyon. Anything and everything seems to be offered in this small-appearing store. (From the front it looks rather small.) Cabins begin at around $35 and top out at $70. This centrally located resort is also famous for its homemade pies, rolls and daily specials in the restaurant.

Scorched Tree Bed and Breakfast

31601 Poudre Canyon Hwy., Bellvue, CO 80512
(970) 881-2817

Facilities: 2 private rooms each with private bath

Services: Full gourmet breakfast, wine and hors d'ouvres in afternoon

Description: Located in Rustic, exactly 31 miles from US 285 and Hwy 14 turnoff, this bed and breakfast appeals to your soft side. Supplying plenty of personal attention and pampering, this is where to stay when in need of that little extra. Rooms are $65 and $80 in this 1925 log cabin.

Mountain Greenery Resort

32595 Poudre Canyon Hwy., Bellvue, CO 80512
(970) 881-2242

Facilities: RV hookups, modern cabins, restrooms, phone

Services: Small general store, gasoline, restaurant, propane water

Description: Located one mile west of Rustic, Mountain Greenery Resort is another mid-river bargain. There's a large shaded area for picnics and a large fine dining area. This spot serves both day boaters and multi-day boaters. Cabins start at $32 for non-kitchened units and top out at $47.

Poudre River Resort

33021 Poudre Canyon Hwy., Bellvue, CO 80512
(970) 881-2139

Facilities: RV hookups, modern cabins, restrooms, phone

Services: Small general store, video store, laundromat, water

Description: Poudre River Resort is located along a beautiful stretch of fishing water. The store caters mainly to fishermen (women and kids, too), but is pleased to service the river running crowd. This resort caters mainly to quiet family types. Peace and quiet are rare commodities, and the Poudre River Resort offers plenty of both.

Sportsman's Lodge

44174 Poudre Canyon Hwy., Bellvue, CO 80512
(970) 881-2272

Facilities: RV full hookups, rustic cabins, modern cabins, showers, restrooms, phone

Services: Convenience store, fishing licenses, hunting licenses, water

Description: Built in 1931 the Sportsman's Lodge has been a tradition for 60+ years. Located at mile marker 79, the Sportsman's Lodge is along the Sleeping Elephant stretch. With fantastic fishing right across the street, the Sportsman's offers the boater many options for overnight facilities. The rustic cabins begin at $30 per night and top out at $50 per night. These cabins come with a wood-cooking stove and shared restroom and shower. The modern cabin runs $50 per night.

RIVER COMPANIES

Boulder Outdoor Center

2510 - 47th, Boulder, CO

(303) 444-8420

Description: BOC is owned and operated by Eric Bader. The company offers full day trips on all sections of the river. They have trips that specialize in the wild and scenic section and overnight trips. They also offer customized trips for individuals and businesses.

Rocky Mountain Adventures

PO Box 1989, Fort Collins, CO

(970) 493-4005 or 1-800-858-6808

Description: Bill Peisner and Dave Costlow are new owners of this established Poudre River rafting company. They offer half day and full day trips on all stretches of the river. They also have plans for some new trips and should be contacted to see what new fun is in store.

The Mountain Shop

632 S. Mason, Fort Collins, CO

(970) 493-5720

Description: The Mountain Shop carries all of the white water gear you could dream about. They also supply river advice and information. An informational and social club that hopes to raise awareness and involvement. Some rentals are also available.

Wanderlust

PO Box 976, Fort Collins, CO

(970) 484-1219

Description: Pat Legel owns and operates this personable company. Pat keeps his trips to the size that they are cozy and comfortable. Wanderlust runs all of the stretches of the Poudre.

A-1 Wildwater

317 Stover Street, Fort Collins, CO

(970) 224-3379

Description: Robert Breckenridge is the owner of Wildwater. They run all of the Poudre stretches. Breck also has a retail area that sells kayaking and river gear. They also rent kayaking and rafting equipment.

JAX Mercantile Store

1200 N. College Ave., Fort Collins, CO
(970) 221-0544

Description: Jim and Nan Quinlan own and operate the "new" JAX. This is a retail store of merit. If you haven't been to visit this impressive store, make sure you make time to see this huge "toy" store. They carry all types of river accessories. Any type of miscellaneous gear you may need can be found here. Enjoy this great store.

Poudre River Kayaks

1524 W. Oak St., Fort Collins, CO
(970) 484-8480

Description: Claire Carren supplies a quality service including: pool, pond and river lessons. Private and group classes. Rentals, custom service, and new and used equipment.

REI

4025 S. College Ave., Fort Collins, CO
(970) 223-0123

Description: Outdoor department store. Everything you would need from whitewater kayaking/canoeing to camping.

Adventure Outfitters

334 E. Mountain, Fort Collins, CO
(970) 224-2460

Description: Excellent deals on new and used backpacking, camping and climbing gear. One place not to miss for deal hunters.

GLOSSARY

Bank scout – Reading the river from the bank or shore.

Big water – Time when the river is near or at peak runoff. Can be a positive thing or a negative thing.

Boulder garden – Set of rocks in the river that creates numerous obstacles. Usually requires navigation to run without mishap.

Bow – Front portion of the boat or what you do after running the Narrows.

Broach – Situation where a kayak is held sideways against a rock. Can cause entrapment within the boat and drowning.

CFS – Cubic feet per second. The amount or volume of water that goes by a point in a segment of time.

Chute – A place in the river where the fewest obstacles are found in a designated drop.

Class I – Still or moving water with few obstacles.

Class II – Small rapids with waves up to two feet.

Class III – Powerful rapids with up to 4-foot waves. Some maneuvering required.

Class IV – Long, difficult rapids with intricate maneuvering and turbulent water. Rescue is difficult.

Class V – Extremely difficult water with violent rapids that require precise moves. Rescue is difficult.

Class VI – Considered unrunnable.

Confluence – The point where two rivers flow together.

Diversion dam – A manmade obstacle that is always deadly.

Drop – What to never do with your paddle, or the place where the river disappears from river view.

D-ring – A steel ring made of steel that is attached to the outside of a raft for securing lines and cam straps to the boat.

Eddy – A calm section of water just downstream of an obstacle. Water flows upstream in an eddy.

Eddy hop – To move up or downstream from eddy to eddy.

Eddy line or fence – The water flowing downstream meets the water flowing back into the eddy and produces counter currents. Difficult to break through at high water levels.

Eddy out – The process of entering an eddy. Boats and swimmers must break through the eddy line.

Ender – The spiritual experience of sending the bow or stern into a hydraulic and getting the kayak or raft vertical.

Eskimo roll – Controlled panic.

Falls – A place where the drop is greater than the horizontal distant run.

Flip – Turning a boat completely over.

Flotsam – Unidentified floating river trash, such as trees, limbs, oars, paddles, swimmers, etc.

Fountain rock – Rock that is strategically placed so the current hits the rock and the water sprays up into the air.

Gradient – The measurement of a river's steepness. Measured in feet per mile.

Hair – What most male kayakers do not have, or the most difficult run.

High side – A paddle and oar boat command to keep the high side of the raft down and prevent either a wrap or a flip.

Hole – Place in the river where the steepness of an obstacle causes the river surface to move back upstream and create low spot(hole) where the water moving towards the river bottom meets the water moving upstream.

Hydraulic – See hole and add adrenaline.

Kayak – A hard-shelled boat which rafters think is for nonsocial deviants and criminally inclined cretins.

Keeper – A hydraulic that will hold you indefinitely.

Oar boat – A raft powered by oars. (duh)

Paddle boat – A raft powered by paddles. (double duh)

Peak run-off – "It was the best of times and the worst of times." C. Dickens. Time when the maximum amount of water is being discharged from snow melt.

Portage – To walk around a rapid.

Pour-over – A hole that is very steep and dangerous.

Put-in – An access point for boats

Raft – A vehicle that kayakers think is for the socially deviant cretins and the mentally disturbed.

Rapid – A place where heaven meets earth or hell has been unleashed.

River left – Left as you look downstream.

River right – Right as you look downstream.

Rooster tail – Water that is flushed together and up as it moves through a fast, narrow passage.

Souse hole – A hole that will not hold indefinitely but does come back on itself.

Stern – Rear portion of the boat.

Strainer – A safety hazard caused by branches or trees in the water. Can be at or below the surface.

Take-out – Exit location from the river for boaters.

Technical – A section of river that requires much maneuvering.

Tour-on – A derogatory term used for people who help support river bums' habits by paying for a raft trip and in turn pays them as raft guides.

Washed out – A '60s kayaker who used too many controlled substances, or when the water level gets high enough so the rapid becomes flat water.

Window shaded – The feeling inside a hydraulic as one goes around for the umpteenth time. Feels and looks like a window shade you let go of too fast.

Wrap – A safety situation where a boat is held sideways against an obstacle and the bow and stern "wrap" around the rock.

SELECTED REFERENCES

Peterson, R.M., 1980, *Cache la Poudre Wild and Scenic River.* Draft environmental impact and study report; USDA. Forest Service, pp4-22.

Wentz, D.A., 1974, *Environment of the Middle Segment, Cache La Poudre River Colorado;* U.S. Geological Survey, pp3-11.

Kingery, H.E., 1987, *Colorado Bird Distribution Latilong Study;* Colorado Division of Wildlife.

Meany, C.A., 1990, *Colorado Mammal Distribution Latilong Study;* Colorado Division of Wildlife and the Denver Museum of Natural History.

Hammerson, G.A., and Langolis, D., 1981, *Colorado Reptile and Amphibian Distribution Latilong Study;* Colorado Division of Wildlife.

Armstrong, D.A., 1972, *Distribution of Mammals in Colorado;* University Museum, University of Colorado.

Evans, Howard Ensign, and Evans, Mary Alice, 1991, *Cache La Poudre: The Natural History of a Rocky Mountain River;* The University Press of Colorado.

Gary Brunner enjoying the Lower Narrows.

PERSONAL RIVER LOG

Date	Entry

PERSONAL RIVER LOG

Date	Entry